Better Homes and Gardens®

APPLIQUÉ

BETTER HOMES AND GARDENS® BOOKS

Editor: Gerald Knox
Art Director: Ernest Shelton
Associate Art Director: Randall Yontz
Production and Copy Editors: David Kirchner, Paul Kitzke
Crafts Editor: Nancy Lindemeyer
Senior Crafts Editor—Books: Joan Cravens
Associate Crafts Editor: Ann Levine
Senior Graphic Designer: Harijs Priekulis
Appliqué Book Designer: Sheryl Veenschoten
Graphic Designers: Faith Berven, Rich Lewis, Neoma Alt West, Linda Ford

CONTENTS

Appliqué is such an exciting and versatile craft, it is fun and rewarding right from the start. To make sure you enjoy learning to appliqué, we have included step-by-step instructions for these simple-to-stitch projects, as well as basic how-to for hand- or machine-stitchery.

To show off your appliqué skills, here are lots of big-impact projects that illustrate how flexible appliqué can be. Complete patterns and how-to make these projects doable and fun.

Each of these appliqué projects has some unusual feature to help you discover new ways of working with fabrics—as well as a new technique to combine with appliqué and add to your expertise.

Patterns from Quilts _____ 68-83

Because appliquéd quilts are part of our American heritage, we have included a collection of favorite patterns for you to make. Some are simple designs, while others are more complex; still others combine appliqué with pieced patchwork. Whatever your level of skill, there is a pattern here that will enable you to share in our quilting tradition.

Creative Appliqué _____ 84-96

Apply all of your appliqué skills and demonstrate your mastery of the stitcher's art with one of these wonderfully exciting and creative projects.

Designer Credits and Acknowledgments _____ 96

Learning to Appliqué

Because appliqué is such a versatile, exciting technique, you will find it fun and rewarding right from the start. To make sure you enjoy learning to appliqué, we have included step-by-step instructions for a variety of fabulous projects. Even a beginner can create the vibrant, attractive floral pillows shown here. Once you have mastered appliqué basics, you are on your way to self-expression in many fabric designs. Lots of quick-and-easy, sure-fire-success projects start you off, and after that, you will be able to combine different patterns and techniques to come up with some great stitchery possibilities. Complete how-to for these machine-appliquéd wildflower pillows starts on page 22.

Appliqué Basics

Appliqué can be as simple as a paper collage or as complicated as a thousand-piece jigsaw puzzle. But however complex the design, all appliqué involves the same procedure— applying one fabric to another. To help you get started on this exciting and challenging craft, here is some basic information on fabrics, cutting and sewing appliqués by hand or machine, and combining appliqué with other needlework techniques such as quilting and embroidery. Use these tips to add a personal touch to the "material" things in your life.

The first step in appliqué is to select a design. Unless you are already skilled in appliqué techniques, this may be the hardest step of all. So choose with care at first, for some designs are easier to stitch than others.

If you are a beginner, select a design with straight lines or gradual curves, and one with a relatively small number of large or medium-sized pieces rather than a trainload of tiny ones.

Next, decide on the technique you will use to secure the appliqué to the background fabric. While it is possible to glue fabrics or fuse them with iron-on webbings, sewing by hand or machine is more secure and, in most cases, more practical.

Then choose fabrics that are easy to sew, and you will have made a good start.

Selecting and Preparing Fabrics

A leisurely trip through a fabric store will unearth a wealth of fabrics for appliqué. Make your selection on the basis of the technique you will use (hand or machine appliqué), care requirements of the article you are making (will it be washed?), and compatibility of the fabrics you want to use together.

Felt is a wonderful fabric for appliqué. It works well with either hand or machine stitching, and because it is non-woven, it will not ravel. So you never need to turn under the edges. It does fade, however, and most felt has to be dry-cleaned.

For hand-appliqué—where you will turn under the edges of the pattern pieces before stitching—choose light- to medium-weight, supple fabrics that are easy to manipulate. One hundred percent cottons (or cotton blends) such as broadcloth, gingham, denim, and sailcloth and lightweight wools are all

suitable. Some knits work well, but if a knit is very stretchy, back it with a scrap of cotton or iron-on interfacing to stabilize it.

For machine-appliqué, you can select from most weights, including upholstery fabrics. Some lightweight fabrics have enough body to sew well. Others, however, need interfacing to stitch well by machine.

Depending on the effect you are seeking, you will find interesting textures for machine work in velveteen, corduroy, homespun, peau de soie, and even vinyl, real leather, and felt.

The basic test for appliqué fabric is this: how easily does a needle slip through the fabric? Wool, cotton broadcloth, and wool felt all sew easily. The fine percales, such as those found in sheets, however, are sometimes difficult to stitch because they are closely woven, with a high number of threads per inch.

Next, how easily does a fabric ravel? Loosely woven fabrics ravel easily, making them hard to stitch by hand. One hundred percent cottons tend to ravel less than blends, making them favorites among quilters.

Evaluate each fabric by itself and in combination with others. For most projects, you will want to use fabrics of about the same weight, care requirements, and durability. For hanging panels, however, the sky is the limit. Mix textures, prints, and colors to get the effect you want.

When buying fabrics, start with the background color. It is easier to develop a whole scheme once you have selected the major color.

Mixing fabrics and patterns is a matter of personal taste. If you are comfortable with a potpourri of prints, use them.

Before cutting pattern pieces, straighten the grain of the fabrics and preshrink them.

Making Appliqué Patterns

After choosing a design for appliqué, enlarge the pattern on a large sheet of paper, following directions on page 67. This is your master pattern.

Make a second pattern to cut apart for the individual design elements. To keep track of the pieces, number or letter corresponding shapes on the cutting pattern and the master pattern. On large projects, jot down the total number of pieces to cut for each shape on the master.

For each shape to be used often in the overall design, make a sandpaper, cardboard, or plastic template that can be traced around many times. For other pieces, make heavy paper patterns. Do not add seam allowances to pattern pieces.

When shapes overlap on the overall design, cut each pattern piece as though it were uninterrupted. For example, if one leaf partially covers another leaf, cut two full leaf patterns, as shown on the diagram at right.

Cutting Pattern Pieces

When laying out patterns for cutting, position large appliqués so the straight grain of the fabric runs the same direction on both the appliqué and the background fabric. This prevents puckering and stretching of the appliqué during stitching or after washing. (The lengthwise grain runs parallel to the selvage of the fabric; the crosswise grain runs at right angles to the selvage.)

With fabric face up, lay out pattern pieces, leaving *at least* ½ to 1 inch between them to allow for seams (see diagram at right).

Trace patterns with a sharp pencil. *The pencil line represents the stitching or folding line, not the cutting line.* Unless directions for your project specify otherwise, cut pieces ¼ inch be-

yond the penciled outline.

If raw edges of appliqué pieces begin to ravel, touch the edges with a dot of white glue. When dry, the glue will be clear and the edge will hold securely.

Sometimes you will need to interface a piece. For machine appliqué, use iron-on interfacing on lightweight fabrics to prevent puckering. Also, if one piece of a pattern will partially cover another and the lower fabric is visible through the upper one, interface the top piece to hide the shadow or cut away the lower fabric after stitching.

For hand appliqué, cut interfacing without seam allowances. For machine appliqué, cut it the same size as the pattern piece.

Appliquéing by Hand

Hand and machine stitching are both "correct" approaches to appliqué. Choose between them on the basis of your project, its intended use, and the fabrics you have selected.

The first step in hand appliqué is to turn under seam allowances on pattern pieces. If desired, machine-stitch along the seam line (¼ inch from raw edges). Clip the seam allowance to the stay-stitching on curves and corners so turned edges lie flat and smooth. Next, baste along the fold of each piece (see lower diagram at right). Or, turn raw edges under as you stitch them to the background.

Sometimes two or more shapes are layered together onto the background; a flower petal, for instance, may overlap a stem. Do not turn under the seam allowance on the lower shape where it will be covered by the upper shape. Instead, clip the seam allowance and tuck the raw edge under the overlap.

Pin and baste the appliqués in place on the background fabric. Then you are ready to stitch.

continued

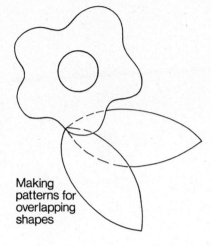

Making patterns for overlapping shapes

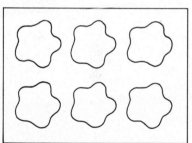

Leaving seam allowances between pattern pieces

Basting seam allowances

Appliqué Basics *(continued)*

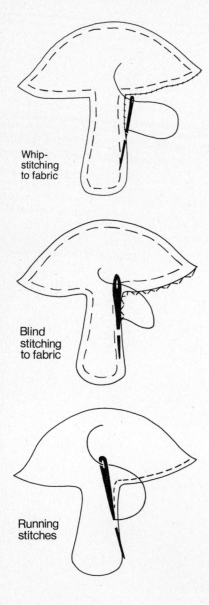

Whip-stitching to fabric

Blind stitching to fabric

Running stitches

Most hand appliqué is based on a variation of a running stitch. The traditional appliqué stitch is the *whipstitch* (see top diagram at left). For this stitch, bring the needle up through the appliqué ⅛ to ¹⁄₁₆ inch from the edge, and reinsert it into the background at the edge of the appliqué, making a small diagonal stitch. Bring the needle up again through the background and the appliqué and continue stitching.

With whipstitching, the edge of the appliqué will be held flat against the background fabric. It is a very secure stitch.

The *backstitch* is similar to the whipstitch in that it makes a flat edge and is very secure.

With the *blind stitch*, stitches are almost invisible in the appliqué piece (see the diagram at left). Bring the needle through the fold of the seam allowance and pick up a thread or two of background fabric at that point. Then pick up a thread or two along the fold of the appliqué. Repeat around the appliqué shape, making stitches about ¼ inch apart. This stitch is also secure, but it gives the edge of the appliqué a soft, puffy look.

The running stitch is often used in hand appliqué. Weave the needle in and out close to the folded edge of the appliqué, taking tiny stitches (see lower diagram at left). When worked in embroidery thread, this stitch is very decorative.

Much appliqué stitching will be along straight edges or curves and will present no problems. *On inside curves and corners*, however, snip the seam allowance so it can be turned smoothly. Then stitch as you would a straight edge, taking a tiny whipstitch where needed to prevent fraying.

To make an outside corner, first stitch one edge up to the hem allowance. Then, using the needle, turn the hem of the second edge under and continue stitching, as shown in the diagram at right.

To make a pointed edge, stitch one edge first. Then, using the needle, turn under the second edge. Make a tiny whipstitch at the tip to keep the corner from fraying (see diagram at right). Then stitch along the second edge.

Machine Appliqué

Most machine appliqué is done on a zigzag machine, although successful projects also can be completed on a straight-stitching machine (see the Rainbow Quilt on pages 24 to 27, for example).

For a straight-stitch machine, cut appliqué pieces with a ¼-inch seam allowance. Stitch along the seam line and clip curves as needed. Press seam allowance under and pin the appliqué piece to the background fabric. Machine-stitch around all edges ⅛ inch from fold.

To make the almost "traditional" machine satin stitch, cut all pieces, allowing at least ½ inch for seams on all sides. Pin appliqué pieces in position on background fabric and hand-baste if desired.

Next, machine-baste. With a short, straight stitch and matching thread, machine-stitch on marked lines. Or set the machine for medium-wide, medium-long zigzag stitches (10 to 12 stitches per inch) and zigzag-baste the appliqué in place. Trim excess fabric beyond the stitching with small, sharp scissors. To finish, set the machine for a zigzag satin stitch and zigzag over the basting on the appliqué pieces, covering the raw edges.

To get the best results, use even hand tension on the fabric. Guide, do not push or pull, fabric—to do so will make the work uneven. If the appliqué puckers, loosen tension.

When the design requires stitching a sharp corner, zigzag up to the corner and leave the needle in the fabric at the outside of the line of stitches. Then lift the presser foot and pivot the fabric. Lower the presser foot and start your stitching so the first stitch goes toward the inside of the design, overlapping the stitch just made. Then continue stitching.

To finish, pull threads to back side and tie off.

If the fabrics you are working with are lightweight and tend to draw during machine-stitching, support them with iron-on interfacing or a piece of organdy under the appliqué.

On highly textured fabrics that do not take a pattern well, work from the back of the background fabric. Do not mark stitching lines on individual pieces, but do mark the overall pattern on the *back* of the background fabric. Next, pin the appliqué in position on the front of the fabric and straight-stitch it in place from the back. Turn the fabric right side up, trim the margin beyond the stitch line, and machine satin-stitch on the front to cover the raw edges of the appliqué.

If your machine has a variety of decorative stitch settings, this is a perfect time to use them. You can richly embellish appliqué with several rows of fancy stitches in matching or contrasting colors. Also try using double needles with different colors of top thread—even metallics—for special effects.

Tools that Help

Good, sharp shears are a must for cutting out appliqués and for keeping fabric edges from fraying. Embroidery scissors are handy for cutting small shapes and for clipping seam allowances along curves.

Also have a supply of sharp,

stainless steel pins and needles available. For hand appliqué, generally the heavier the fabric, the larger the needle you will need. For machine work, keep needles in various sizes on hand. Change needles regularly—dull ones are hard to stitch with.

Cotton or polyester thread works well for hand- or machine-stitching. Also try threads made for machine stitchery. Or use silk thread for a shiny, rich appearance.

Fusible webbings are valuable too, for a bit of webbing can hold a small appliqué piece in place better than a pin.

Appliqué Plus

There are numerous ways to embellish appliqué work, but the most commonly used ones are quilting and embroidery.

For traditional quilting, add batting and backing fabric to your appliqué and then hand- or machine-quilt in outlines around the appliqués, in blank areas between them, or within the appliqués themselves. Add dimension to individual appliquéd shapes with trapunto quilting— open the background fabric and add padding between the background and the appliqué. Many of the projects in this book call for quilting, since it is an integral part of much appliqué work.

If you want to use embroidery in combination with appliqué, try buttonhole stitches worked around the edge of the appliqué. They are not only decorative, but can be used in place of whipstitches to anchor the appliqué to the background fabric.

For textural interest, try French knots or a variety of raised stitches on the surface of your appliqué. Do not hesitate to experiment freely with embroidery stitches—they will make all of your appliqué projects uniquely your own.

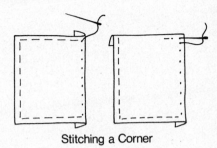
Stitching a Corner

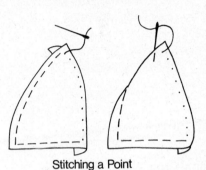
Stitching a Point

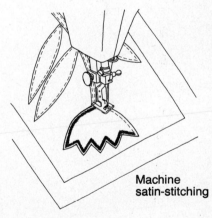
Machine satin-stitching

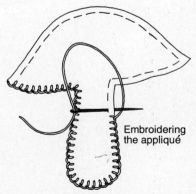
Embroidering the appliqué

Quick-and-Easy Heart Pillow

Our simple heart pillow has just one shape hand-appliquéd onto the background fabric four times. With gradual curves and both an inside and an outside corner on each heart, this pillow is a great project for a beginner. And hand-quilting gives this pillow old-fashioned charm.

Materials

⅓ yard white or off-white cotton fabric
¼ yard red print fabric
¼ yard green print fabric
12-inch square of lining
12-inch square of quilt batting
White or off-white quilting thread
Polyester fiberfill

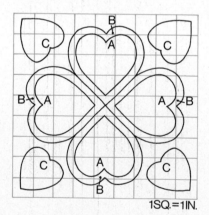

1 SQ. = 1 IN.

Directions

Note: Finished size is 11½ inches square.

Cut a 9¾-inch square from the white fabric. Cut 4 hearts (A) from the red print fabric and appliqué them to the white square as shown on the pattern, turning the raw edges under ¼ inch. Use whipstitches for a flat edge on the appliqué or blind stitches for a rounded edge.

Cut four 1⅝x11¾-inch strips from the green fabric. With right sides together, sew 1 strip to each side of the square, using ¼-inch seams. Miter the corners and clip excess material. Press seams to one side.

Cut a piece of lining and a piece of quilt batting to match the pillow top. Baste the three layers together, from the center to the edges, with the batting in the middle. Quilt around the appliquéd hearts, staying as close to the edge as possible. Take tiny running stitches and go through all three layers.

Using a hard lead pencil, *very* lightly draw around each appliquéd heart, using heart B as a pattern. Lightly draw around heart C four times, placing 1 heart in each corner, as shown on the pattern. Be sure to mark lightly, since the lines may not wash out completely. Quilt around each of these traced designs. Remove basting.

Cut a piece of white fabric to match the front, and with right sides together, sew the front to the back using a ¼-inch seam. Leave an 8-inch opening in one side for turning. Turn right side out and stuff. Slip-stitch the opening closed.

Quick-and-Easy Bird Pillow

This pillow design also is worked in gradual curves, but here you will get a chance to work with several layers of appliqués, fitting them together to form a graceful bird. A pieced patchwork border accents the appliquéd motif.

Materials

12½-inch square of dusty rose fabric
9¾-inch circle of white fabric
½ yard navy fabric
Fabric scraps in shades of green, purple, rust, coral, pink, and orange
Polyester fiberfill

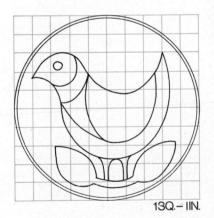

13Q. – 1IN.

Directions

Enlarge the pattern and cut out pieces, referring to the photograph for colors. Fit smaller pieces onto large body piece of bird; turn under raw edges and appliqué in the following order: neck band, breast, wing, and eye. The edges of the throat, breast, and wing pieces should overlap so they barely touch when appliquéd.

Pin the bird, the bird's feet, and the leaves in place on the white circle. Tuck the feet under the body and leaf stem so that when edges are turned under, they will not expose raw edges of feet. Appliqué the bird's body onto the white circle.

Center the circle on the 12½-inch square and appliqué it in place. Edge the square with a border of 1-inch-wide navy blue strips, using a ¼-inch seam. Also using a ¼-inch seam, cut and piece random fabric scraps to make four 1½-inch-wide strips, referring to the photograph for color ideas. Piece the strips until they're long enough to go around the blue border. Press seams to one side. With right sides together, sew these strips to the navy strips in a ¼-inch seam. Finish the pillow front with navy strips sewn to the multi-colored strips. Cut these navy strips any width (1-inch-wide strips make a 15-inch pillow) and sew them to the striped border.

Cut a piece of navy fabric to match the pillow front, and with right sides together, sew the back to the front, leaving a 12-inch opening in one side. Turn, stuff, and slip-stitch the opening.

Quick-and-Easy Wall Hanging and Pillow

To create these contemporary views of nature, use simple shapes, bold colors, and trapunto quilting in combination with machine appliqué.

Materials

Scraps of velveteen, brushed corduroy, and broadcloth in rust, copen blue, brick red, orange, gold, white, and medium and light shades of gray-brown, red-brown, and green
Two 20x16½-inch pieces of navy blue broadcloth (pillow)
20x18 inches plum-colored cotton (wall hanging front)
20x18 inches printed flannel (wall hanging back)
½ yard iron-on interfacing
Pillow stuffing
Blue and red thread
Curtain rings

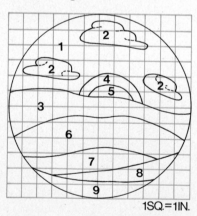

1 SQ. = 1 IN.

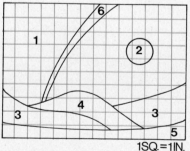

1 SQ. = 1 IN.

Directions

Wall Hanging

Enlarge the pattern at left below, following directions on page 67. Cut individual pattern pieces from fabric, referring to the photograph for colors. Cut the top half of the circle as a single brick red shape and appliqué clouds and sun pieces onto it. Add a ½-inch margin to pieces after lightly marking the seam line with pencil or dressmaker's carbon paper.

Cut matching shapes from iron-on interfacing and fuse interfacing to the wrong side of each piece. The interfacing should give the fabric enough body to keep it from puckering when it is stitched. If it does pucker, adjust thread tension on the sewing machine. Trace a 12-inch circle in the center of the plum-colored fabric.

Appliqué the shapes in the circle as follows: Pin a shape in position, following the numerical sequence on the pattern. Next, machine-baste on the seam line of the appliqué with a narrow-width, medium-length zigzag stitch (10 to 12 stitches per inch). Use red thread. (The bobbin thread should not be visible on the face of the fabric; if it is, adjust tension.) With sharp scissors, trim excess fabric beyond the stitching line.

Reset sewing machine for wide, closely spaced zigzag stitches (machine satin stitches); sew again over outlines of each appliqué, covering raw edges. Pin and machine-baste all pieces in place before doing any of the final stitching. Then satin-stitch all outlines at the same time—*except the outline of the circle*, which is satin-stitched later. Add wisps on clouds with felt pen.

To quilt the shapes in the appliquéd scene, turn the fabric wrong side up and make small slits in the background fabric behind each shape except the clouds. Be careful not to cut into the appliqué itself. Lightly stuff the shapes, using an orange stick to tuck stuffing into tight corners. Then slip-stitch the slits closed.

To assemble the wall hanging, cut two 4x4-inch squares. Cut each one in half across the diagonal and machine-baste one triangle to each of the corners of the plum-colored fabric as shown in the photograph. Do not satin-stitch yet, Next, with right sides together, stitch the back of the wall hanging to the front, leaving an opening for turning. Turn right side out and stuff lightly. Slip-stitch the opening. Then machine satin-stitch along the diagonals of the corner triangles and around the circle. Sew curtain rings to upper corners for hanging.

Pillow

Enlarge the pattern at left and cut out the pattern pieces, referring to the photograph for colors. Cut the green velveteen as a single piece and appliqué the arc and circle onto it. Fuse iron-on interfacing to backs of pieces. Mark a 10½x14-inch rectangle in the center of one of the pieces of navy fabric, and appliqué the shapes onto it in numerical order, following directions for the wall hanging. After machine-basting, satin-stitch all edges, including the outline of the large rectangle.

Quilt all of the shapes on the pillow except the copen blue arc (piece #6), following directions above.

To assemble the pillow, baste and then stitch the pillow front to the back, right sides together. Leave an opening for turning. Turn, stuff the pillow, and slip-stitch the opening closed.

Quick-and-Easy Window Shade

This machine-appliquéd window shade will make your child purr with delight. Machine embroidery accents our lion, while wooden trim turns the window into a circus wagon.

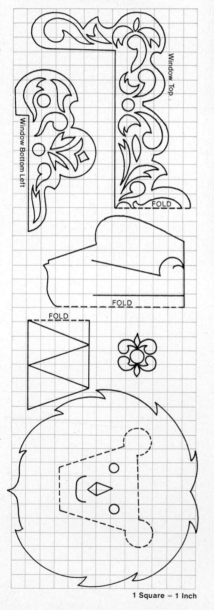

Window Top

Window Bottom Left

FOLD

FOLD

FOLD

1 Square = 1 Inch

Materials

2 yards dark fabric for shade
¼ yard white fabric
¾ yard yellow and red print fabric
8 yards ½-inch-wide red ribbon
1½ yards yellow adhesive-backed paper
½ sheet ¼-inch plywood
Red semigloss paint
Roller and hardware for shade
Wooden dowel

Directions

Enlarge the patterns at left, reversing the bottom left window piece to make the bottom right piece. Cut window trim and two 12-inch circles (wheels) from plywood. Paint red. Glue or nail pieces to window along outer trim. Nail 1x3-inch lumber below window trim. Attach wheels. Paint window trim red.

Cut yellow design details from yellow paper; attach to wood.

Install the shade roller and cut shade fabric to fit window. Turn a 1½-inch hem at bottom of fabric to make a casing for the dowel. Hem sides of shade.

Cut lion pieces from fabric, referring to the photograph for colors. Appliqué them to the shade with machine satin-stitching. Machine-embroider design details with dark thread. Finish by sewing ribbon bars over the lion.

Quick-and-Easy Game Banner

If your family loves games, you'll find this banner practical as well as decorative and creative. Make it with fabric scraps, ribbon, and bits of trim.

Materials

Blue, green, and red printed and
  solid corduroy or other
  medium-weight fabric
Ribbons and buttons for trim
Curtain rod
Blue fringe

Directions

Note: Finished size is approximately 72x45 inches, but can be adapted to fit any wall space.

Cut two pieces of blue corduroy to desired size; with right sides facing, sew sides together in a ½-inch seam. Insert fringe along the bottom and sew the pieces together. Turn right side out; turn under ½ inch at top. Cut seven hanging tabs and decorate with ribbon, as shown. Fold each tab in half (to make a loop), and insert between the two layers along the top edge. Sew the pieces together in a ½-inch seam, making sure no raw edges show.

Make chess and other game boards, cutting all the pieces from fabric scraps and using the photograph as a guide. Machine-appliqué the pieces in place so that each board is complete. Attach the boards to the background with nylon fastening tape.

Add decorative details to fill in the rest of the background. Cut fabric letters to spell out the name of each game, and add ribbons and buttons for trim. Hang from a curtain rod.

Quick-and-Easy Baby Quilt

Here's a delightful way to use fabric scraps— machine-appliqué this 44x58-inch crib-size quilt. Preshrink the fabrics before you begin. Then appliqué the blocks and set them together with gingham strips. Tie the top to a layer of padding and backing for a speedy, economical, and practical gift for baby.

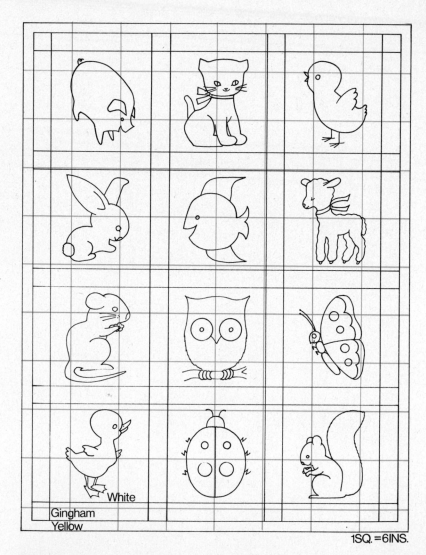

1SQ.=6INS.

Materials

4¼ yards 44-inch-wide white cotton
5¾ yards 44-inch-wide yellow and white gingham
¼ yard yellow cotton
1 crib-size package of quilt batting
Scraps of small cotton prints, ginghams, and solids in bright colors
Yellow yarn
#5 black pearl cotton
White quilting thread

Directions

Enlarge patterns and cut pieces from fabric, using the photograph opposite as a color guide. Appliqué design details onto each animal. Then cut twelve 12½-inch white squares. Center one animal on each square and appliqué in place with machine satin-stitching. Embroider small details with black pearl cotton.

To assemble the quilt, cut nine 2½x12½-inch gingham strips. Using ¼-inch seams, sew three strips between four blocks to make each row. Cut four 2½-inch strips the length of the rows; sew between rows and at sides of quilt. Cut and sew strips to top and bottom.

Cut batting and backing to match quilt top. Sandwich batting between top and backing, pin and baste the layers together, and quilt around the animals with white thread, if desired. Bind edges of the quilt with 1½-inch-wide yellow bias strips. Tie yarn through all layers and at intervals along gingham strips.

Quick-and-Easy Animal Toys

These enchanting appliquéd pillow toys trace their ancestry to the pottery of the Mimbres Indians of the Southwest. This ancient tribe was renowned for its early development of ceramics and its use of mythical and exaggerated figures — much like our fanciful interpretations of the antelope, quail, turtle, and insect.

Materials
Polyester fiberfill

Turtle
¼ yard dark green suede cloth
⅛ yard light green suede cloth
Dark green crewel yarn

Insect
¼ yard purple corduroy
¼ yard striped cotton fabric
Gray and blue-gray crewel yarn
Light brown suede cloth

Quail
⅓ yard beige crinkle cloth or other cotton fabric
⅛ yard chocolate brown suede cloth
Beige crewel yarn

Antelope
⅓ yard coral suede cloth
Light brown, medium brown, and pumpkin suede cloth
Medium brown crewel yarn

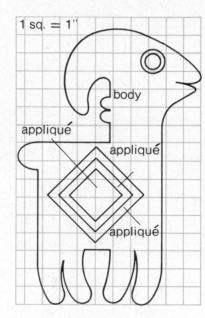

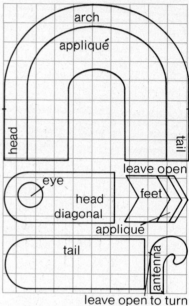

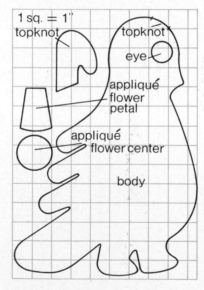

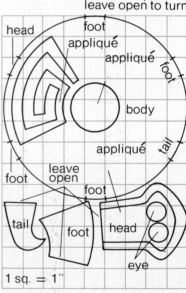

Directions
Enlarge pattern pieces and cut them from fabric, using the photograph as a color guide. Turn under raw edges of design details ¼ inch and appliqué in place. Embroider eyes with yarn French knots. With right sides together, sew small body pieces — head, tail, or feet — using a ¼-inch seam, leaving an opening. Turn right side out and stuff moderately. Machine-stitch the small body pieces to the front of the animal, then sew front to back body pieces, leaving an opening. Turn, stuff lightly, and slip-stitch.

Quick-and-Easy Coverlet and Pillowcases

Chic and contemporary, this soft supergraphic comforter is also a snap to stitch. Made from only four pieces of fabric, it's a dream of a machine-appliqué project. And if you machine-quilt it too, you can make this coverlet in just one day.

Adapt the motif to fit a pair of pillowcases for a bedroom full of pizzazz.

Materials

2 yards each of white, black, and brown cotton (44-inch-wide)
4 yards white fabric (backing)
Quilt batting
Brown and white quilting thread
Black thread
Purchased pillowcases
³/₈ yard each of black and brown fabric (pillowcases)
Scrap of rust-colored cotton

Directions

Enlarge the pattern below and cut the central motif from black fabric, adding ¼-inch seam allowances. Machine stay-stitch on the seam line of the black circle and strip. Then press under the seam allowance, clipping the curves so edges are smooth.

Lay the white fabric flat. Pin the black strip over one long edge so the center of the inside rim of the black semicircle is ¼ inch above the raw edge of the white fabric. Baste. Center the black circle 1 inch inside the semicircle; pin and baste. Appliqué the circle and strip to white fabric.

Lay out brown fabric, and position lower edge of black strip along one edge. Pin, baste, and appliqué in place.

Cut backing fabric in half and sew together along one long edge, making a piece 89x72 inches. Assemble the coverlet, following directions on page 71. Outline-quilt by hand or machine in rows 1½ inches apart. Stop quilting 1 inch from the raw edge of the coverlet.

Turn raw edges to the inside ½ inch; slip-stitch.

For the pillowcases, repeat the quilt motif on one case. On the other, appliqué a rust-colored circle to a black and white pillowcase, as shown opposite.

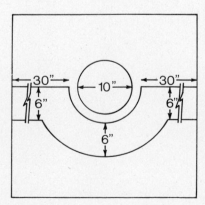

Quick-and-Easy Wildflower Pillows *(shown on pages 4 and 5)*

For a bright splash of color in your living room make just one or all eight of our wildflower designs shown on pages 4 and 5. Machine-appliqué the basic shapes to a slightly textured background fabric, add machine-embroidered details, and stitch and stuff the covers into large (20-inch-square), dramatic pillows.

If leisurely hand-appliqué is more your style, you can still stitch up these beautiful pillows—we tell you how on the next page.

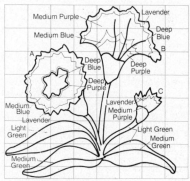

Bachelor's-button

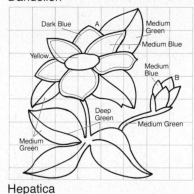

Dandelion

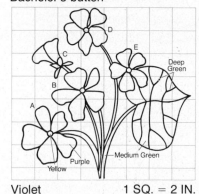

Violet 1 SQ. = 2 IN. Hepatica

Materials
(for each pillow)
²/₃ yard 44-inch-wide white Haitian cotton or any similar closely woven, medium-weight fabric
Scraps of fabric in colors suggested in color key
Thread to match fabrics
Iron-on interfacing
Polyester fiberfill or 20-inch pillow form
90 inches cotton cable cord

Directions
Enlarge patterns above and opposite. To add body to the fabrics and to help prevent puckering when they are stitched, fuse iron-on interfacing to wrong side of fabric scraps before cutting. Cut pattern pieces following the color guide, opposite. Add ½-inch seam allowances if you are appliquéing by machine.

Machine-appliqué in place small detail pieces such as flower centers before appliquéing flowers to pillow fronts.

For machine appliqué, follow these steps: Pin the piece to be appliquéd in position. With the sewing machine set for a medium-wide, medium-long (10 to 12 stitches per inch) zigzag stitch, baste around the edges of the appliqué with matching thread. Trim excess fabric beyond the stitching line. Reset the machine for wide, closely-spaced zigzag stitches and stitch around edges again, covering basting and raw edges with a neat line of machine satin stitches.

If fabric puckers or bobbin threads show on the surface of the fabric, adjust tension on spool and bobbin threads.

Arrange flowers on 22-inch squares of white fabric, positioning the appliqués so the lengthwise grain of the background fabric will run the same direction on all the pillows. Pin the flowers in place. Next, pin leaves and stems in place, tucking raw edges under flower petals, if necessary. When everything is in place, machine-baste (zigzag stitch) the pieces to the pillow and remove the pins.

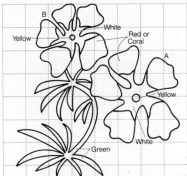

Gilia

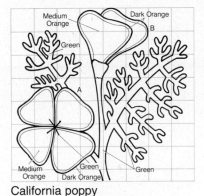

California poppy

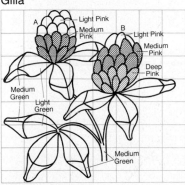

Clover

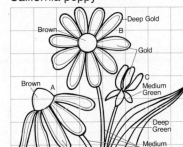

Black-eyed Susan

Color and Cutting Guide

Bachelor's-button: Flowers A and B are blue; flower C and center of flower A are lavender appliqués. Work details in purple thread. Cut and appliqué leaves and stems as a single piece.

Dandelion: Flower A is a solid yellow with deep yellow stitching; flower B is yellow with an orange appliqué center and deep yellow stitching. Cut and appliqué leaves and stems as a single piece with deep green stitching and veins.

Violet: Appliqué each flower as a single unit with yellow appliquéd center. Cut and appliqué leaf and stems as a single piece; outline veins and details of petals in satin stitches.

Hepatica: Cut and appliqué flower and bud as single pieces; appliqué leaves and stems individually. Use matching thread for details on flowers and leaves.

Gilia: Cut and appliqué flowers, yellow centers, and stem and leaf sections as single pieces; outline white portion of each petal with white thread.

California poppy: Cut and appliqué flowers A and B, stems, and leaf sections as single pieces; outline individual petals on flowers in satin stitches.

Clover: Lower half of each flower is deep pink, upper half is medium pink. Work appliqué and details in deep pink thread. Cut and appliqué stems and leaves individually; work details in deeper green thread.

Black-eyed Susan: Petals and centers of flowers A and B are cut and appliquéd individually and outlined with a deeper shade of thread. Flower C and leaf/stem unit are each cut as single pieces and details are outlined with satin stitching.

Sketch interior design details onto the fabric shapes with chalk and machine-embroider over the chalk lines using the same wide satin stitch used for the appliqués. Press the fabric.

Cut and piece 1½-inch-wide bias strips of green fabric. For each pillow, cover 90 inches of cotton cable cord with the bias strips using a zipper foot and matching thread. Pin and sew the cording to the front of the pillow 1 inch from the raw edges. Round the corners. Where ends of cording meet, fold under raw edge of cording fabric to form a clean edge.

Cut a 22-inch square of white fabric for the pillow back, making sure grain line runs the same direction as on the front. With right sides together, sew the front and back pieces together in a 1-inch seam. Leave an opening for turning. Trim seams and clip corners; turn right side out and press. Stuff the cover with polyester fiberfill or a pillow form and slip-stitch the opening closed.

To hand-appliqué the wildflower designs on the pillows, enlarge the patterns, adding ¼-inch seam allowances to all pieces. Cut stems on the bias so they can be curved easily. Cut pieces from fabric, turn under the seam allowance on each, and baste along the fold. Hand-appliqué small shapes to flowers before stitching flowers to pillow fronts, as above. Then hand-appliqué flowers, stems, and leaves to pillow fronts. Hand-embroider interior design details.

Assemble the pillow covers following directions above.

Displaying your Skills

To show off your appliqué skills, here is a big, splashy, easy-to-stitch rainbow quilt that any stitcher would be proud of. In this section, you will find lots of colorful, big-impact projects designed to illustrate just how flexible appliqué can be. For instructions for making this quilt, stitched entirely by machine, please turn the page.

Rainbow Quilt *(shown on pages 24 and 25)*

Bursting with color, this rainbow quilt is made with fabric shapes that are machine-appliquéd into separate blocks. Each block is then quilted individually and sewn to an adjoining block with yellow binding to hide all raw edges.

Materials

Note: All fabric is 45 inches wide.
1¼ yards blue fabric
3⅔ yards yellow fabric
3½ yards red fabric
10 yards green fabric
Quilt batting (80x90-inch size)
Thread

Directions

Construct each block of the quilt separately, beginning with the largest one (top left in the diagram opposite) so you can use excess material for smaller blocks. After the tops of the blocks are appliquéd, assemble each one (with batting and backing fabric) and quilt it. Sew blocks together into three large pieces and sew large pieces together to make the complete quilt.

Enlarge the pattern opposite onto newsprint or brown paper.

When cutting pieces from fabric, add a ¾-inch seam allowance to all four sides of the blocks (background pieces) and a ¼-inch seam allowance to the outer, curved edges of the semicircular pieces. Read instructions below before cutting out any pattern pieces.

For each block, cut a square for the back from green fabric; set it aside. Cut quilt batting to size; set aside. Using the same pattern and following the color key, cut a square for the quilt front. Then cut semicircles from the appropriate-colored fabrics. *Do not cut the centers from the semicircles.*

Press under ¼ inch along the curved edge of all semicircles. Position the largest semicircle on the front piece. Topstitch it along the curved edge close to the fold using matching thread.

After stitching, trim excess fabric from *underneath* the curved edge of the appliquéd semicircle for use in other blocks. Topstitch the next largest semicircle in place in the same way. Continue appliquéing semicircles until the block is completed. *Trim away excess fabric from beneath semicircles only after the next piece has been topstitched in place.*

When all the blocks are appliquéd, assemble the green backing fabric, batting and appliquéd front for each one. Sandwich the batting between the front and back pieces of each block and pin the layers together about every 3 inches along the semicircular shapes. Machine-quilt just outside each semicircle using thread that matches the color of the fabric.

To assemble the quilt, cut yellow fabric down the length in five 1½-inch-wide strips (18 yards total). Stitch blocks together as explained below and in the numerical order indicated on the pattern. Join blocks into three large pieces as shown on the pattern, then stitch these large sections together in the same way.

To join two blocks, first cut a yellow strip the length of the seam (measure the actual blocks before cutting). Lay two quilt blocks together with the green sides (backs) facing. Place the yellow strip on top, with all raw edges even. Stitch together in a ½-inch seam and trim the seam allowance to ¼ inch.

Pull the blocks open; lay them flat. *Gently* press yellow strip toward seam, covering raw edges (too much heat or pressure will flatten batting). Topstitch strip along the fold. Turn under ½ inch on remaining edge and topstitch to adjoining block.

Finish the edges of the quilt by binding them with yellow fabric: Cut three strips down the length of the fabric, each 2¼ inches wide (to equal 9⅔ yards). With raw edges even, sew yellow strips to the back of the quilt in a ½-inch seam. Press binding to the outside and topstitch close to the edge on the quilt back. Then bring the strip to the front, turn under ½ inch on the remaining raw edge, and topstitch to the front, making sure the fold on the front hides the first two seams along the edge. Turn under the ends of the yellow strips at the corners of the quilt or stitch them together into a mitered corner.

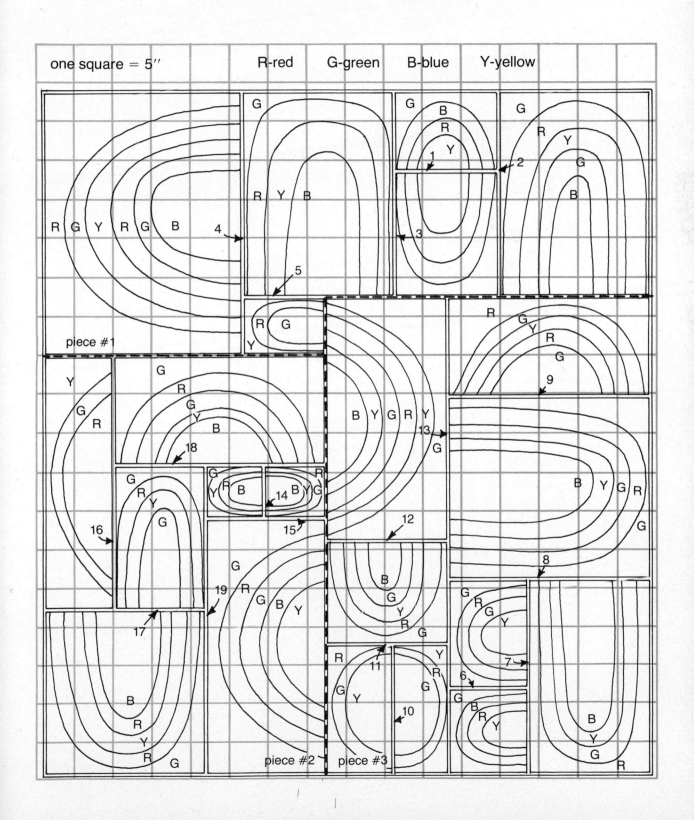

Appliquéd Garden Scene

Create our "enchanted garden" wall hanging with only snippets of delicate floral fabrics. To make this delightful project (also pictured on our cover), appliqué your pretty prints onto a floral background. Then add embroidery details to give the scene a rich, lively appearance. The quilted picture, which measures 14x19 inches, is a charming way to display your stitchery.

1SQ.=1IN.

Materials

6x20 inches blue and white floral print (sky)
8x20 inches green and white floral print (ground)
½ yard print fabric (backing and border)
8x10 inches muslin (house)
Scraps of floral prints, with motifs that are ¾ inch to 1 inch in diameter (shrubs, flowers)
Green, red, orange, blue, lavender, yellow, and brown embroidery floss
White cotton thread
Dressmaker's carbon
Three 18x20-inch pieces of quilt batting
¼x14x19-inch piece of plywood

Directions

Turn under the seam allowance (¼ inch) on one long edge of the ground fabric and topstitch it to one long edge of the sky fabric, making the background for the scene. Appliqué or embroider the remaining design details onto this main piece.

Enlarge the pattern and transfer outlines to the background. Use outlines as placement guides for individual motifs.

Cut backing same as front. Sandwich batting between front and back pieces and baste layers together. Using two strands of white thread, quilt the ground in horizontal rows and the sky in semicircles, spacing rows and stitches ½ inch apart.

Cut muslin for house 1 inch wider and 3 inches higher than pattern. For clapboard siding, sew ¼-inch tucks in the fabric. Press raw edges under ¼ inch; appliqué in place. Cut roof and shutters, adding seam allowance. Fold under raw edges; appliqué. Cut and sew muslin squares over shutters (windows). Using two strands of blue floss, embroider windowpanes. Add a muslin chimney.

Embroider the evergreens in vertical rows of green satin stitches.

Cut shrubs and flowers from floral prints, adding seam allowances. Turn under edges and arrange them on the front, referring to the photograph opposite if necessary. Appliqué green floral shrubs along the horizon and around the house. Position clusters of flowers in front of the shrubs. For sunflowers (upper right), appliqué a ½-inch-circle (add seam allowances) of brown print fabric to the background. Then satin-stitch yellow triangular petals around the center; add embroidered green stems and leaves.

Embroider a monarch butterfly hovering near the sunflowers. Add embroidered flowers among the appliquéd flowers, and embroidered stems and leaves on some appliquéd blossoms.

Frame the picture with a 2½-inch border of floral fabric slipstitched to the sides. Mount on plywood, as shown.

Appliquéd Staircase Scene

A companion piece to the garden scene on page 29, this quaint appliquéd interior scene is also accented with quilting and embroidery. If you are thrifty with your fabric scraps—saving small pieces from previous projects—you'll probably have on hand everything you need to make this charming panel.

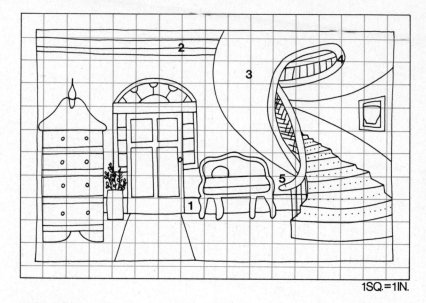

1SQ.=1IN.

Materials

5x20 inches rust print (floor)
10x20 inches rust and beige print (wall)
½ yard print (backing and border)
¾ yard unbleached muslin
Scraps of brown fabric
Scraps of floral prints in green, blue, brown, and tan
Three 15x20-inch pieces of quilt batting
Brown, green, gray, and yellow embroidery floss
White quilting thread
15x19-inch piece of ⅜-inch plywood

Directions

Turn under ¼ inch on long edge of the floor piece and stitch it to the wall piece, making the background. Cut backing to match, and sandwich batting between front and back. Baste layers together and quilt, spacing rows and stitches ½ inch apart.

Enlarge the pattern to use as a cutting and positioning guide. When cutting pieces for appliqué, add a ¼-inch seam allowance.

First, appliqué the molding strips (1 and 2 on the pattern). Cut base molding (1) from muslin, turn under raw edges, and appliqué along seam between floor and wall. Cut ceiling molding 3 inches deeper than the molding on the pattern and take two tucks in it before appliquéing it along the top of the wall.

Cut staircase (3) from a double layer of muslin. Turn under seam allowance, appliqué, and quilt. Add muslin trim (4) to edge of staircase. Appliqué brown print banisters (5). Embroider stairs in outline and running stitches. Add gray floss posts.

To make the bureau, appliqué a brown rectangle in place. Add the feet of the bureau, then the top and drawer struts. Finish with satin-stitched finial (at center top) and drawer pulls.

For the window and door, cut window arch and sides from muslin (in one piece) and appliqué. Add blue print windows. Over this, stitch door, a narrow strip for the lintel over the door, and door panels. Add white embroidered windowpanes and a black doorknob.

Cut out, appliqué, and quilt the runner in front of the door.

For the sofa, appliqué green print "upholstery" first, then embroider legs and edging in brown satin stitches. Add green embroidered outline stitches to mark the front and back of the seat on the sofa. Appliqué a tiny round pillow to the back.

Appliqué a fabric vase and fill it with embroidered yellow flowers. Finish with an appliquéd picture on the wall: sew down a brown patch, then a muslin patch, and finally, an appliquéd flower.

Edge the scene with a 1½-inch border of printed fabric and a 3-inch muslin border. Mount on plywood.

Swan Pillow and Curtains

Our beautiful black swan is appliquéd onto a pillow and then enlarged and adapted for a curtain panel. Each piece of the design is sewn down with running stitches worked in pearl cotton—an unusual and attractive appliqué technique.

Materials
Pillow
15-inch circular pillow form with 2-inch boxing
28-inch circle of black cotton
13-inch circle of white cotton
1x41 inches green bias strip
10-inch circle of heavy dacron quilt batting
Scraps of light blue, dark green rust, brown, and coral cotton
#5 pearl cotton in colors to match fabric

Curtains
8 yards 45-inch-wide black cotton (see note at right)
4 yards white cotton
½ yard dark green cotton
½ yard light blue cotton
¼ yard brown cotton
Scraps of coral cotton
#5 pearl cotton in colors to match fabrics

1 SQ.=1IN.

Directions
Pillow
Enlarge the pattern below and cut out pieces, referring to the photograph for colors. Add ¼-inch seam allowances to all pieces.

Turn under seam allowances on all pieces; baste. Pin and baste pieces to white circle. Using pearl cotton to match fabrics, appliqué pieces with small running stitches along the edges. Turn under and baste a ½-inch hem in the white circle.

Fold green bias strip in half lengthwise and pin behind white circle, letting ¼ inch of the folded edge show along the front. Join ends of the strip and baste in position.

Using black pearl cotton, sew basting stitches ½ inch from edge of black circle; gather the circle. Slip pillow form inside circle, centering it. Draw fabric up around pillow form, spacing gathers evenly. Place batting over empty space inside black fabric. Center and pin appliquéd white circle over batting. Appliqué the edge of the white circle to black fabric; sewing through all layers. Finish by embroidering the eye of the swan with black pearl cotton.

Curtains
Note: Fabric requirements are for two 36x58-inch curtains, each lined and interlined to minimize fading. To make curtains of a different size or without interlinings, adjust fabric amounts.

First make a drawing of the curtain (it need not be full-size). For each curtain, draw a rectangle and mark it 36 inches wide and 58 inches long. On the inside and lower edges of each curtain, mark a 5-inch-wide black border. In the upper outside corner, mark a black rectangle 19 inches wide by 41 inches long. The white, appliquéd panel is an L-shaped piece 12 inches wide that fits between the outer border and the inner black rectangle (see photograph). On the diagram, mark the vertical length of the white panel (53 inches on the outer edge; 41 inches on the inside) and its horizontal dimensions (31 inches on the lower edge; 19 inches on the upper, inside edge).

Add ½-inch seam allowances to all dimensions and cut out pieces. Cut the L-shaped white panel double so black lining and interlining will not show through. Instead of cutting it as an L-shaped piece, cut the outer 5-inch border (black) in a single strip and miter the lower inside corner.

Enlarge the swan motif to 1½ times the size for the pillow, adding extra leaves and a fourth cattail to the design and extending the stems on the cattails and the blue waves, as shown in the photograph. Reverse the swan motif for the second curtain.

Cut out pattern pieces and appliqué them to the white panel, following instructions for the pillow. Embroider the swans' eyes.

To assemble the curtain fronts, baste inside hems in black strips (along edges that will be joined to white panels). Appliqué them to white panels, matching seam lines.

For hanging loops, cut five 32½x5-inch pieces of black for each curtain. With right sides facing, stitch long edges together in a ¼-inch seam. Turn right side out and press. Fold tabs in half and space them evenly across top of curtain front with raw edges even. Baste.

Cut black lining and interlining to match fronts. Layer interlining, lining, and curtain front (wrong side up). Pin and stitch layers together, catching tabs in seam. Leave bottom edge open. Turn, press, and slipstitch lower edge, turning in seam allowance.

Machine Appliquéd Crèche Banner

Appliquéd by machine and featuring touches of machine embroidery, our contemporary Christmas crèche measures 30x50 inches. Make yours to fit any wall space you choose.

1SQ.=1IN.

Materials

2¼ yards drapery-weight muslin
2¼ yards polyester quilt batting
1½ yards fusible webbing
1½ yards red fabric
½ yard yellow fabric
½ yard white fabric
½ yard red calico fabric
1 yard purple polka dot fabric
Scraps of pink, purple, red, orange, and blue fabric
Red and black sewing thread
1 skein black embroidery floss
8 yards red hem tape
Tissue paper
Brown wrapping paper

Color Key

Pink	P
Red-orange	RO
Orange	O
Purple	PL
Dark orange dot	DOD
Light orange dot	LOD
Red	R
Maroon	M
Pink-purple	PP
Yellow-orange	YO
Orange calico	OC
Lavender	L
Pink dot	PK
Purple dot	PLD
Light beige	LB
Yellow	Y
Black	B
∿∿∿∿ = stitching colors	
Black	b
Red	r
White	w

Directions

Enlarge the pattern and transfer to paper. Cut pieces without seam allowances—they will fit together flush, like a puzzle.

From white fabric, cut the infant (including head, halo, and Mary's hands). From red, cut Mary (including head, halo, and arm). From purple, cut Joseph. Using fusible webbing to hold pieces, appliqué smaller shapes to main pieces. Lightly pencil-in facial features and drapery lines. Zigzag-stitch design details, following the pattern. Appliqué finished pieces to the background. Add the manger. Fray pieces of yellow fabric (straw) and fuse in place. Baste quilt batting to the back and quilt. Bind edges with red hem tape, and stitch tape to back top for hanging rod.

Festive Rejoice Banner

You'll feel like rejoicing when you hang this colorful appliquéd banner. The mood it evokes is especially suited to Christmastime, but the exuberant message is a welcome sight all year.

To simplify construction, iron the letters to the muslin with fusible webbing to hold them in place for machine satin-stitching.

Materials

2½ yards natural-colored drapery fabric or medium-weight muslin for background
2½ yards white lining fabric
Pieces of broadcloth in various colors and prints for vertical stripes and letters
3 packages 2-inch-wide red hem tape
Fusible webbing
Matching thread and embroidery floss
Curtain rod

Directions

Note: The finished size of the banner is 84x30 inches.

Cut drapery fabric or muslin background piece to measure 84x32 inches. Also cut a matching lining piece.

Enlarge the pattern below. Cut the vertical stripes from broadcloth and pin them to the background material. Machine- or hand-appliqué around the edges. Turn a ¼-inch hem if you appliqué by hand; trim the raw edges if you machine-appliqué.

Cut the seven letters from broadcloth, referring to the photograph for color suggestions. Arrange the letters on the stripes and baste them in place. Appliqué with tiny whipstitches if you are sewing by hand.

Or, iron the letters in place with fusible webbing and stitch them down with machine zigzag stitching or another decorative machine embroidery stitch.

Gently press the finished banner front on the wrong side.

Machine-stitch a length of hem tape to the top of the lining piece, ½ inch from the raw edge. Then stitch the remaining long edge of the tape to the lining to make a casing. Do not stitch ends.

Sew the lining to the back of the muslin, using a ½-inch seam.

Pin hem tape around edges, folding it in half to cover the edges, and slip-stitch in place. Insert a curtain rod for hanging.

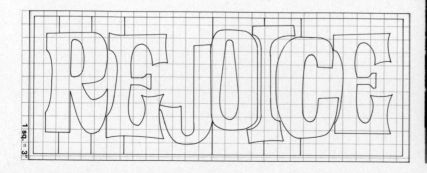

1 sq. = 3"

Appliquéd Bird Quilt and Pillows

The striking appliquéd comforter and pillows shown here are the natural habitat for a rare flock of fantastical birds. Though you may never see this group of fine feathered friends gathered together in an honest-to-goodness tree, for the appliqué artist, anything is possible.

This lively contemporary quilt and the matching pillows can be either machine- or hand-stitched.

Materials

Note: All measurements refer to 44- or 45-inch-wide cotton broadcloth

5 yards brown for tree trunk, branches, and border strips

2½ yards beige for border strips

1⅔ yards dark green for leaves and ground

2 yards medium green for leaves and ground

2 yards white with brown polka dot

¼ yard black

¼ yard rust

⅛ yard each of red, purple, navy, gold, pink, off-white, gray, and medium blue

5 yards matching or contrasting fabric for backing

2 packages 96x96-inch quilt batting

#5 pearl cotton in the following colors: gold, rust, black, purple, navy, red, blue, gray, pink, medium green, dark green, brown, and white

Basting thread

Graph paper

Transfer pencil or dressmaker's carbon

Quilting hoop or frame

Directions

Note: The quilt shown above and opposite is 86 inches square. The center appliquéd square (without borders) is 58x58 inches. Change the size of the quilt by varying the size of the borders.

Directions for the four appliquéd pillows shown with the quilt, opposite, are on pages 40 and 41.

Preshrink all the fabric. Enlarge the pattern on page 40 for the appliquéd center panel and transfer it to a large sheet of brown paper. This will be the master pattern.

Trace each separate shape on the quilt (birds, tree trunk, and branches) onto a separate sheet of paper and cut out all paper pattern pieces. Select a single complete leaf shape and make one leaf pattern for all 76 leaves. Number all pattern pieces to correspond to the shapes on the master pattern.

To construct the basic background for the quilt top, lightly trace the outlines of the top half of the background onto the polka dot fabric and cut out, adding ½-inch seam allowances all around. Next, trace off the dark green ground piece and cut out, adding ½-inch seam allowances. Baste under the seam allowance along the top edge of the green ground piece; pin and baste to the bottom of the polka dot piece, overlapping seam allowances. Repeat for the medium-green ground piece.

continued

Appliquéd Bird Quilt and Pillows *(continued)*

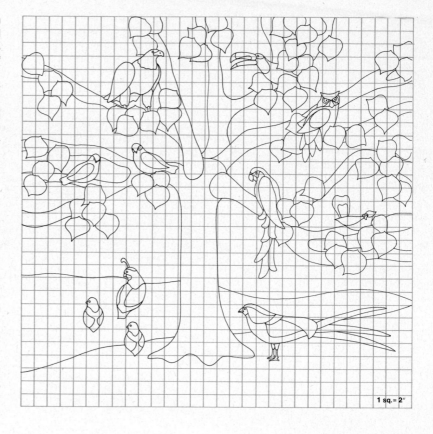

1 sq. = 2"

Place your master pattern on top of the pieced background fabric and lightly trace outlines of the tree shape, birds, and leaf placement onto the background. Use a transfer pencil or dressmaker's carbon paper.

Next, cut out all the trunk and branch shapes from brown fabric, adding ¼-inch seam allowances to each piece. Carefully turn under all seam allowances and baste. Then pin and baste trunk and branches in place on the background fabric.

Cut 33 dark green and 43 medium green leaves, adding ¼-inch seam allowances. Turn under seam allowances, baste, and press. Arrange leaves on tree trunk and branches following the master pattern. Trim excess fabric where leaves overlap; pin all leaves in place.

Finally, cut out and assemble pieces for each bird, working on one bird at a time. Place all bird and leaf pieces in position before sewing to ensure that raw edges are properly covered. Trim away excess fabric where necessary.

When all pieces of the quilt have been pinned or basted in position, appliqué around the edges of each one, taking small running stitches in matching pearl cotton ⅛ inch from all folded-under edges. (Or, slipstitch appliqué pieces in place with matching sewing thread.)

Where indicated on the pattern, embroider beaks, eyes, and talons in satin stitches, using gold, black, or rust pearl cotton.

To assemble the quilt, cut two 4-inch-wide strips of brown fabric and machine-stitch to the top and bottom of the appliquéd panel with ½-inch seams. Repeat with two 4-inch-wide brown strips along the sides of the panel, squaring the corners.

Next, add 11-inch-wide strips of beige fabric to the top and bottom of the quilt panel, and then to each side of the panel (again using ½-inch seams). Press all seams toward outside edges of the quilt.

Piece backing to size from a sheet, muslin, or from matching or contrasting fabric.

Cut two layers of batting to size. Lay the backing fabric wrong side up on the floor, spread two layers of batting on top, then add the quilt top, face up, on top of batting.

Align all the edges, then pin and baste through all layers; use long stitches running diagonally from corner to corner and through horizontal and vertical centers. Mount on a quilting hoop or frame, if desired.

Stitching through all layers, use white pearl cotton to outline-quilt around all shapes on the polka dot background. Then use dark and medium green thread on the ground areas, following all seam lines and quilting around the base of the tree trunk. Next, quilt around each bird on the ground. Finally, quilt along the inner and outer edges of the dark brown border.

Trim the backing and batting so the outside edges are even with the edges of the top. Cut four long pieces of 2-inch-wide brown fabric; sew one strip to each edge of backing fabric (½-inch seams).

Turn under raw edges of brown fabric, press, and fold this binding strip to the front of quilt. Baste to quilt top, then sew through all layers with dark brown pearl cotton, securing binding to the quilt top.

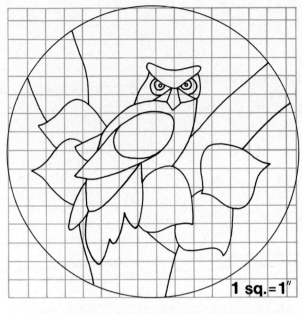

1 sq. = 1"

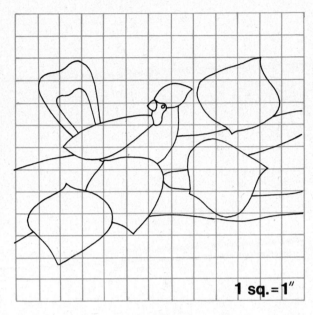

1 sq. = 1"

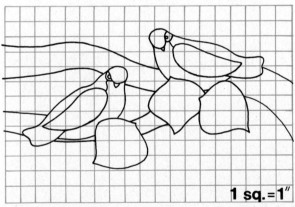

1 sq. = 1"

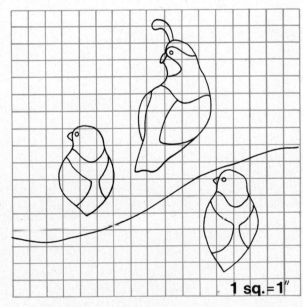

1 sq. = 1"

Pillows

Enlarge the patterns on this page. Cut out and appliqué the pieces onto circular or rectangular pillow fronts, following the instructions for sewing the quilt top. To enhance the designs, trapunto-quilt individual shapes on the birds, following directions on page 48.

To complete each pillow, cut backing fabric to size. Stitch it to the pillow front, right sides together, leaving an opening for turning. Turn the cover right side out, stuff, and slip-stitch.

Special Appliqué Techniques

In this section, you will find appliqué projects "with a difference." Each one has some unusual feature to help you discover new ways of working with fabrics. Our tablecloth, for instance, is worked in shadow appliqué— a technique for using sheers. Here also are designs for hand- or machine-stitching in padded, shaped, or embroidered appliqué, lacework, and reverse appliqué—all exciting techniques. For tablecloth how-to, turn the page.

Shadow Appliqué—Tablecloth and Napkins

(shown on pages 42 and 43)

Shadow appliqué is the creative art of stitching with sheers. For this technique, one sheer fabric is appliquéd atop another, or a heavier fabric is appliquéd to the underside of a sheer or between two layers of transparent fabric (as in our wall panels on pages 46 and 47). The look is soft and delicate—like a shadow.

The organdy tablecloth shown on pages 42 and 43 is appliquéd by hand in the traditional pin stitch—a pulled-thread embroidery technique. It creates a decorative line of holes similar to hemstitching—but unlike hemstitching, this stitch works beautifully on curves.

If you are a fan of old-fashioned needlework, you will want to add this technique to your repertoire.

Materials

44x44 inches soft, sheer, white cotton organdy or lawn
1 yard soft, sheer, beige cotton organdy or lawn
¼ yard each of lightweight cotton broadcloth in pale pink, pale yellow, and pale green
¾ yard white batiste or fine handkerchief linen (4 napkins)
Gray cotton embroidery floss
Small tapestry needles
Black felt-tip pen
Tissue or brown paper

Directions

Enlarge the patterns for the border and the central motif, opposite. Tape together enough tissue or brown paper to make a piece 44 inches square. Then transfer to the paper the patterns for the central motif and border and go over the outlines with a felt-tip pen. This is your master pattern. Lay the sheer fabric over it to be sure appliqués are in position.

Transfer the outlines of each shape to the fabrics indicated on the pattern by laying the pressed fabric over the master pattern and lightly marking the outlines with a hard pencil. Cut out the appliqués, adding ¼-inch seam allowances. Except on the beige border that extends around the cloth, turn under the seam allowance on each shape, baste close to the folded edge, and press. Then trim the seam margin to about ⅛ inch. On the border piece, turn under and baste only the seam allowance on the curved (inside) edge. The straight (outside) edges will be sewn to the edges of the white organdy piece later, after smaller pieces have been appliquéd.

Lay the white organdy over the master pattern and pin and baste the appliqués in position on the right side of the fabric. Where appliqués meet, lap flower petals over stems and leaves (except at the bases of the flowers, where the stems should overlap the flowers slightly). To overlap, remove the basting on the piece to go underneath along the area of the overlap. Clip into the seam allowance with scissors and pull it out flat. Then lap the top piece over it.

Appliqué pieces in position with tiny pin stitches, pulling the thread tight with each stitch to make a line of decorative holes around each appliquéd shape.

To make pin stitches, use a single strand of embroidery floss in a small, blunt tapestry needle. Work with the fabric firmly in hand so you can pull on the thread. Slide the thread end under the appliqué (out of sight). Bring it up at A in the background fabric right next to the appliqué (see the stitch diagram, opposite). Take a tiny backstitch (¹⁄₁₆ inch or smaller), and bring the needle up again at A. Pull the thread tight to create a tiny hole in the fabric, and take a second backstitch. Bring the needle up again in the appliqué fabric directly above A; pull the thread tight. Reinsert the needle at A and bring it up again at B, ¹⁄₁₆ inch or less ahead. Repeat this double backstitching and catch-stitching around the appliquéd shape, securing it to the fabric.

When all parts of the central motif have been appliquéd with pin stitching, add embroidery to the design. Use tiny backstitches for the dotted lines on the pattern, and satin stitching and French knots or seed stitches in the centers of the green flowers, as shown in the photograph on pages 42 and 43.

Work the border by first stitching the beige border appliqué to the background fabric (right sides together) around the outside (straight) edges. Use a ¼-inch seam. Press the appliqué to the front of the white organdy and pin and appliqué the curved edges, leaves, and flowers in position.

To make the napkins, cut fabric into four 15-inch squares. One-half inch from the edges of the fabric, mark curves as shown in the photograph on pages 42 and 43. Machine satin-stitch along design lines and trim excess fabric beyond the stitching. Using part of the motif from the center of the cloth, appliqué a flower, leaves, and stem in one corner of the napkin. Follow directions above for pin-stitching.

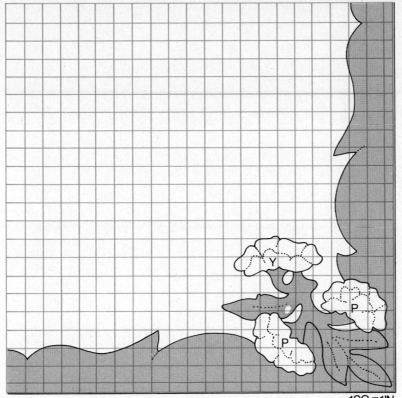

1SQ.=1IN.

Color Key

Y   Yellow
P   Pink
G   Green
W   White
B   Beige

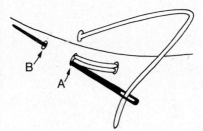

Pin Stitch for Shadow Appliqué

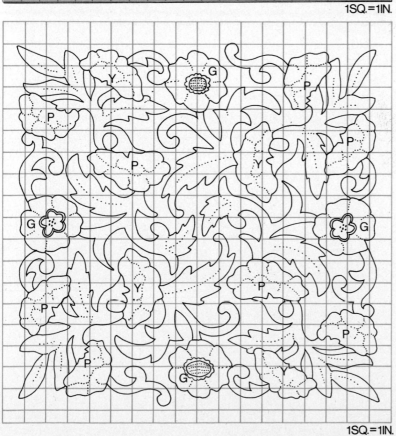

1SQ.=1IN.

Shadow Appliqué—Wall Panels

With another technique for shadow appliqué— using sheer organdy to encase bright-colored felt—you can create muted tones like the ones in these "stained glass" wall panels. Machine stitching holds the layers together and adds the "leading" in the design.

Try this interesting technique and see what exciting results you achieve.

Materials

Sufficient organdy or other
   transparent fabric to cover
   length and width of each
   panel twice (see note)
½ yard green felt
⅓ yard gold felt
Thread in matching and
   contrasting colors
Wood molding

Directions

Note: Measure the wall area you wish to cover and divide it into panels. Our panels are each 2 feet wide and 7 feet tall. To adjust the size to fit your wall, shorten or lengthen at the bottom.

Use the pattern below, or choose a stained glass design consisting of flat areas of color. Draw the design on brown paper. Cut shapes from felt, referring to the photograph for colors.

For each panel, cut two pieces of organdy. Lay one on a table or on the floor, wrong side up, with the brown paper pattern underneath. Position the felt pieces, leaving space for rows of stitching between them. Felt pieces should not overlap. Lay the other organdy piece right side up on top of the felt pieces. Pin and baste through all thicknesses.

Machine- or hand-stitch around each felt piece. Use matching or contrasting thread, or a combination of the two. Remove basting and press lightly with a warm iron.

Tack panels in place on the wall and cover the raw edges of each one with painted wooden molding cut to size.

|← Each Panel 2 Feet →|

Quilted Appliqué—A Soft Brass Headboard

Quilted appliqué — called trapunto-quilting — is the technique of sewing two pieces of fabric together, cutting the back piece open, and stuffing the appliquéd shape to give it dimension. It is often used in conjunction with regular quilting (padding with batting between top and bottom layers of fabric) for a look that is soft and plush, but with areas of high relief.

The trapunto-quilted brass headboard shown here is a simple project to get you started on this easy and exciting aspect of appliqué. On the next four pages are pillows and a wall hanging as well.

Materials

1⅔ yards 45-inch-wide print fabric (background and binding)
1⅓ yards solid-color fabric
1¼ yards gold fabric
Dacron quilt batting
#5 pearl cotton in gold
#5 pearl cotton to match background fabric
Dressmaker's carbon

Directions

Cut a 12x44-inch piece from the print fabric and set it aside. Enlarge the pattern below and transfer it, centered, to the remaining printed fabric. Then trace pattern pieces onto a separate sheet of paper and cut them from the gold fabric. Follow the straight grain of the material and add a ⅜-inch seam allowance.

Turn under seam allowances and pin pieces to the background.

Using gold pearl cotton, appliqué the pieces to the background with small, even running stitches close to the folded edges of the appliqué pieces. Overlap all raw edges.

For trapunto-quilting, cut slits in the *background fabric only* behind each appliquéd piece (do not cut into the gold fabric). Using scraps of batting, lightly stuff the appliquéd pieces. If necessary, use an orange stick to push stuffing into small spaces. Whip-stitch the slits closed.

Cut solid-color backing fabric and quilt batting to size and pin them to the back of the front piece, with batting in the middle. Pin the layers together and quilt around the appliqué, using pearl cotton to match background fabric.

Cut and piece 90 inches of 1½-inch-wide bias binding from the extra print fabric. Fold the long edges under ¼ inch and sew to the raw edges with pearl cotton.

Sew a 2-inch-wide strip just below the top of the quilt in back. Insert an adjustable curtain rod and hang from wall hooks.

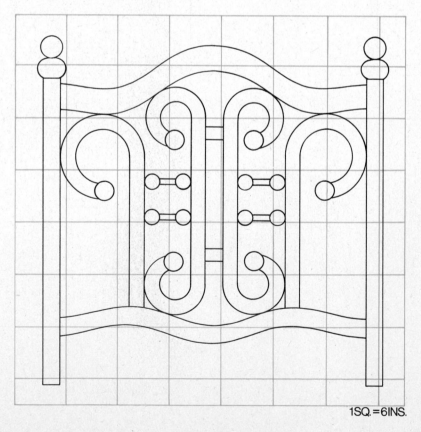

1SQ.=6INS.

Quilted Appliqué—Indian Pillows

Traditional American Indian symbols are machine-appliquéd to the front of these pillows and then given extra shape with trapunto quilting. Machine embroidery complements the distinctive designs.

Materials
1 yard dark cotton or
   cotton-blend fabric
1 pound polyester fiberfill
½ yard unbleached muslin
Black cotton thread
Fabric scraps in assorted solid
   colors
¼-inch-wide cording
Orange stick
Tracing paper

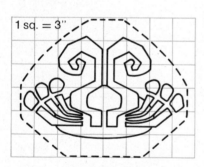

1 sq. = 3"

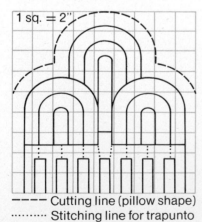

1 sq. = 2"

- - - - Cutting line (pillow shape)
········· Stitching line for trapunto
    over same color

Directions
Enlarge the pillow designs onto tracing paper and draw two complete patterns — one for cutting the pattern pieces and one to use as a placement pattern.

Cut 23-inch-square front and back pillow pieces from dark cotton. Also cut one muslin piece the same size. Do not cut out pillow shapes until fronts have been appliquéd and quilted.

Cut the appliqué pieces from the fabric scraps, using the photographs above and on the next page as color guides.

Layer pillow pieces in the following order: muslin, pillow front, large appliqué pieces, medium pieces, and small pieces. Follow the pattern for placement. Pin the layers together.

Baste each appliqué in place diagonally from corner to corner and then straight-stitch ⅛ inch inside the raw edges. Start sewing in the center of each pillow and work toward the edges.

Machine-appliqué the pieces with close zigzag or satin stitching and black thread. Cover the raw edges completely. Then machine-stitch a narrow black line ⅛ inch inside each side of the satin-stitched

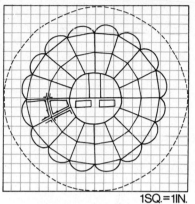

1SQ.=1IN.

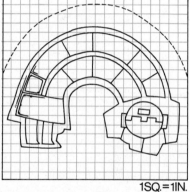

1SQ.=1IN.

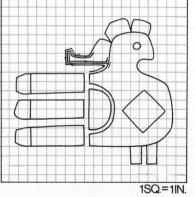

1SQ.=1IN.

lines, following the contours of the appliqué pieces. Create slubs (slight irregularities) along shadow lines by machine-stitching four or five times over ¼-inch areas of each shadow line (see photographs above). Place the slubs randomly along the shadow lines.

For trapunto quilting, cut a small slit in the muslin lining of each appliqué piece (do *not* cut through the pillow front). Pad each shape through the slit with stuffing (do not overstuff or the pillow will look warped). Use an orange stick to push the stuffing into the corners. Whipstitch the slits closed.

When padding is finished, cut the front and back pillow pieces to the appropriate size, following dotted lines on the placement pattern.

Cut and piece 1½-inch-wide bias strips from dark cotton until they are long enough to go around the pillow. Cover cording with the bias strip, and baste to the pillow front ⅜ inch inside the raw edge.

With right sides facing, sew the front and back pillow together in a ⅜-inch seam. Leave at least an 8-inch opening for turning. Turn and press, very gently (too much heat will flatten padding material). Stuff to desired fullness and blindstitch the opening.

Quilted Appliqué—Wall Hanging

Our silhouette in white is an introspective study of a farm wife at work. To make this wall hanging, sew appliqué pieces in place from the wrong side of the background fabric and then trim excess fabric away from each of the body shapes. Finish with machine satin stitching and hand-embroidered accents.

Materials

White or off-white fabrics in 5 or 6 different weights and textures, such as upholstery fabrics and loosely-woven linen:
    1¼ yards (A) (see diagram)
    ¾ yard (B)
    ½ yard (C)
    ½ yard (D)
    ¼ yard (E)
1 yard quilt batting
Matching thread
Natural-colored or ecru silk buttonhole twist
Four 34-inch artist's stretcher strips
Stapler and staples
Dressmaker's carbon or transfer pencil

Directions

Enlarge the pattern and transfer it (centered) to the *wrong* side of a 40x40-inch piece of background fabric (A). Be sure to reverse the design when you transfer it so it will be right side up on the face of the fabric.

Appliqué each pattern piece to the front of the background in the following order: left arm, spoon handle, right arm, face, head covering, bodice, bowls, and fingers.

Do not cut out pattern pieces before appliquéing them. Instead, pin each piece to the face of the fabric, matching grain lines. Turn the fabric over (wrong side up) and straight-stitch along the pattern line for that piece. Then trim excess appliqué fabric close to the stitched line. Stitch and trim each piece before proceeding to the next one.

Using buttonhole twist, machine satin-stitch around each appliquéd piece, covering raw edges. Satin-stitch dotted lines on the bodice also.

For quilting, cut a slit in only the background fabric behind each appliquéd piece. Cut batting to fit inside each piece and insert between the two layers. Whipstitch the slit closed.

Assemble stretcher strips and staple the fabric to the frame. Using buttonhole twist, embellish the neckline, upper arms, bodice front, and thumb with hand-embroidered outline stitching. Embroider through the appliqué only—not through batting or backing.

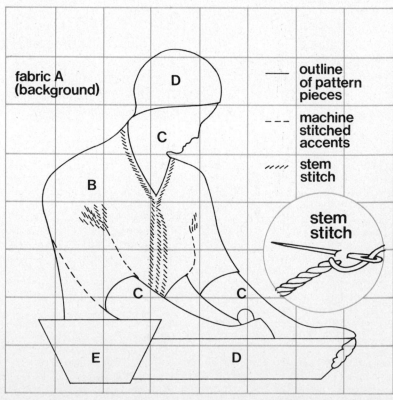

——	outline of pattern pieces
- - -	machine stitched accents
/////	stem stitch

1 Square = 4 Inches

Lace Appliqué—Gift Box

New life for old lace—that's the secret to these next three projects. The satin gift box shown here, for example, is embellished with small pieces of fine antique lace cut from doilies and a tablecloth. Each design is appliquéd with tiny backstitches tucked into the lace itself to completely hide them from view.

Materials

⅔ yard satin or cotton sateen (or any medium-weight fabric with a close weave)
⅔ yard lining fabric
Cardboard for pattern
Mat board
Quilt batting
Lace, ribbon, or other decorative trims
Beeswax

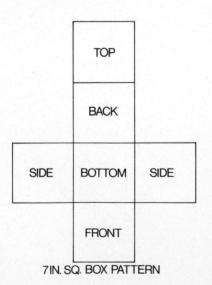

7 IN. SQ. BOX PATTERN

Directions

For a 7-inch-square box, cut a 7-inch cardboard square (template). Trace six template patterns onto wrong side of lining fabric, leaving space between squares for ½-inch seams. Cut out squares, adding seam allowances. (Change box size by changing template size.)

Sew lining squares together, as shown at left. Cut out satin squares and stitch together. Press all seams open.

Appliqué lace or other trims to the satin. Use a thread that matches the lace, and sew with tiny back- or running stitches that anchor the lace snugly to the background fabric.

With right sides together, sew lining to satin, leaving open the bottom of the front square. Turn; press carefully.

Cut ¼ inch off two adjacent sides of the cardboard template. Using this as a pattern, cut six squares from mat board. Slip a square into the open end of the front piece; slide to top of box. Stuff small pieces of batting between mat board and fabric. Stuff corners firmly.

Using a zipper foot, stitch seam line between top and back.

Slide a mat board square into the back piece and repeat the stuffing procedure, then stitch. Do the same with each section until all the squares are stuffed. Slip-stitch opening closed.

Pin corners of side sections to the front and back sections to form a box. Pull thread through beeswax and slip-stitch the box together along its four corners.

Lace Appliqué—Butterfly Wall Panel

Organdy and lace combine beautifully in this butterfly wall panel. For an off-white tint, soak the lace pieces in strong black coffee for thirty minutes before you begin.

Materials

1 square yard white cotton organdy

Two 10½-inch-diameter lace doilies for upper wings

Two 7-inch-diameter lace doilies for lower wings

9 assorted lace circles or ovals for body, antennae, and lower wing tips (see note below)

#3 and #5 ecru pearl cotton

Four 33-inch artist's stretcher strips

Graph paper

Tracing paper

Ecru sewing thread

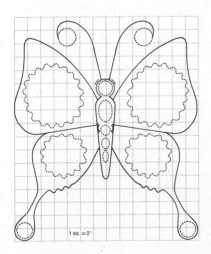

1 sq. = 2"

Directions

Enlarge the pattern, reversing it to complete the design. Tape the pattern to a table and center organdy over it.

For upper and lower wings, pin four large doilies to the fabric (indicated by dotted lines on pattern). Pin lace to the fabric for body, antennae, and wing tips. Using ecru thread, baste around outlines of wings and bodies. Using small, hidden stitches, sew lace to fabric around the *outer* edges.

Turn the fabric over and carefully cut an opening behind the large doilies and the wing tips to within ½ inch of the lace edge. Turn fabric under ¼ inch and sew edges to the lace. Do not cut the fabric behind the body and antennae appliqués.

Using #3 pearl cotton, outline wings with couching: lay the thread along the outline and overcast with ecru sewing thread. Then stem-stitch along outer edge of couching with #5 pearl cotton.

Using #3 pearl cotton, outline body and head with long-armed featherstitches, filling inner edge of outline with longer "spokes."

Embroider antennae in open chain stitches with #5 pearl cotton.

For butterfly eyes, work a line of five French knots following the curve of the head (see pattern diagram). Add three short straight stitches to the lower body, as shown in the photograph.

Cover organdy with a press cloth and iron with low heat. Turn up a ¼-inch hem on raw edges, and frame on stretcher strips.

Lace Appliqué—Quilt

If you have a collection of beautiful lace doilies, dresser scarves, antimacassars, or even place mats, you will find our lace appliqué quilt a wonderful way to display them creatively. Appliqué each piece to a square of cotton broadcloth that can be assembled into a 22-inch square. Next, stitch squares together into a quilt large enough for a queen-size bed. To finish this elegant but practical sampler of treasured handiwork, add a wide lace border (ours came from the edge of an old tablecloth) and decorative hand embroidery.

Materials

4 yards 44-inch-wide cotton/polyester fabric in assorted colors
5½ yards matching or contrasting fabric for backing and border
2 large sheets quilt batting
Twelve 14- to 16-inch round or square lace or crocheted doilies or antimacassars, or any combination of large and small doilies (as shown in the photograph)
10 yards 4-inch-wide old or new lace edging
#5 pearl cotton in white and ecru

Directions

Note: Finished size is about 78x100 inches. Seams are ½ inch.

Wash and preshrink all fabric. Repair old lace with matching thread and wash in cold water and mild soap (no bleach). Do not use delicate or very old pieces of lace since they wear quickly.

Arrange lace pieces to your satisfaction in four rows of three pieces (or groups of pieces) each. Then select backing fabric to complement each grouping of lace. Cut fabrics into squares and rectangles that can be joined into 22-inch squares. (Add seam allowances to all pieces.) After appliquéing lace to fabric, stitch three squares together into a row; then join four rows to make the top. When cutting the fabric squares, keep in mind arrangement of colors.

Begin by centering lace on squares. To make sure the lace lies flat on the fabric squares, press it lightly, then carefully pin it in place. Then stretch the fabric in an embroidery hoop and appliqué.

Appliqué lace in place with matching thread. Take tiny whip-stitches or running stitches so the appliqué blends with the design of the lace. Appliqué in just enough places to hold the lace securely.

If your lace pieces and doilies are too small or too plain for the fabric squares, try adding a bit of embroidery — such as French knots, open chain stitches, or straight stitches — to help make the lace look larger or more decorative.

When all lace is appliquéd, assemble the quilt top by sewing squares together. Press seams to one side. Featherstitch over seam lines using pearl cotton thread.

Add 8-inch-wide border strips around the perimeter of the quilt and appliqué lace edging to the border. Cut the backing material and quilt batting 1½ inches narrower than the quilt top on all sides. Center the layers beneath the quilt top and tuft through the layers at the corners of each 22-inch square, using pearl cotton.

Fold raw edges of the border to the back side, turn raw edges under, and slip-stitch to backing.

Caring for Lace

Handmade lace, old or new, requires special attention in order to preserve its beauty and keep it in good condition. Here are some tips to help keep lace as fresh as the day it was made.

Make any needed repairs before washing the lace, stitching carefully and always inserting the needle *between* the threads, not into them. Using a small, blunt tapestry needle will help prevent split threads. To repair holes, weave horizontal threads as for darning; then, weave in and out of these threads to duplicate the design.

Gently wash the repaired lace in sudsy water, being careful not to rub or squeeze. Rinse the lace and wrap it in a towel, then block it on a fabric-covered board until dry (at least overnight). When blocking, use stainless steel pins to avoid rust.

If stubborn stains persist, treat with diluted lemon juice or hydrogen peroxide, or have the stains treated professionally.

Avoid molding and yellowing by storing lace in a cool, dry, dark place. Lay pieces flat with a layer of tissue paper between.

Shaped Appliqué—Floral Pillows

Here is another way to add dimension to your appliqué work in addition to quilting: shape the appliqué as it is sewn to the background fabric, gathering and pleating it into soft folds. The floral pillows opposite are appliquéd in just this way. For each one, cut small pieces of ribbon (the "petals" on our flowers), gather the edges, and shape the petals as you stitch.

This is truly individualized appliqué — for every flower you make, like every flower in nature, will be unique.

Materials (for each pillow)
1 yard light yellow velveteen
1½ yards cotton cable cord
1 skein each of #3 pearl cotton embroidery thread in light, medium, and dark green
Embroidery needles
Polyester fiberfill

Pansy Pillow
½ yard 2-inch-wide dark purple velvet ribbon
¼ yard 1½-inch-wide light purple velvet ribbon
¼ yard 2-inch-wide dark magenta velvet ribbon
1 skein each of velvet or cotton embroidery thread in light and dark yellow
Thread to match ribbons

Hydrangea Pillow
1 yard 2-inch-wide light blue grosgrain ribbon
½ yard 2-inch-wide medium blue grosgrain ribbon
Thread to match ribbons

Directions

Cut two 16-inch circles of velveteen for each pillow. From the remaining fabric, cut and piece bias strips to cover the cording for the edge of the pillow front.

Enlarge the patterns opposite and transfer them to tissue paper. Trace each one onto the front of one of the circles of fabric, using dressmaker's carbon paper and a tracing wheel or pencil.

Cut the ribbon into 2-inch lengths. For each petal, turn under the raw (cut) edges of the ribbon ¼ inch and press lightly on the wrong side. Be careful not to crush the nap on the velvet ribbon. Do not turn under the finished edges of the ribbon.

Using thread to match ribbons, sew tiny running stitches along one finished (unfolded) edge of the ribbon. Pull up the gathers but do not tie them off.

Begin making flower petals by whipstitching the *ungathered finished* edge of the ribbon to the outside edge of a petal outline marked on the pattern. Whipstitches should be close together to hold the appliqué firmly in place.

Next, pull the folded edges of the ribbon around to follow the outlines for the sides of the petal and whipstitch them in place. Remember that petal outlines are round or triangular and ribbons are not. Also, ribbon pieces are larger than petal shapes. So, while stitching each ribbon in place, shape it to fit into the outlines of the petal by gathering and folding all but the top edge, which will have been whipstitched along the outside of the shape. Lift up each ribbon in the middle of the petal shape to get it out of the way while stitching the side (folded) edges in place.

To finish each petal, arrange the gathered edge of the ribbon along the lower (inside) edge of the petal shape and whipstitch in place. The ribbon will be bunched and folded in the middle of the petal. Tuck a few tiny stitches (that go through the background fabric) underneath the folds in the ribbon to anchor them.

Follow directions below for the order of stitching for each pillow.

To complete each pillow, baste the covered cording to the pillow front 1 inch from the raw edge. With right sides together, sew the pillow front to back, leaving an opening for turning. Clip the curves, turn the pillow cover right side out, and stuff. Then slip-stitch the opening.

Pansy Pillow

Begin by appliquéing the #1 petals to each flower, referring to the photograph for colors. After stitching the top and sides of each petal, pull the gathered edge of the ribbon snug and anchor it in the center of the flower with a few stitches. Add the side petals (#2 and #3) and then the light-colored petal (#4) in the same way. Complete the petals by adding a few small stitches inside of each one to hold the folds and tucks in the ribbon.

Add straight-stitched accents to the petals with light and dark yellow thread radiating from the center of the flower. Cover the raw edges of the ribbon in the center of the flower with three or four large French knots, wrapping the thread around the needle five or six times for each one.

Using light, medium, and dark shades of green pearl cotton, embroider the stems in satin stitches and the leaves in close herringbone stitches. Then complete the pillow, following directions above.

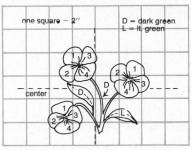

one square = 2"

D = dark green
L = lt. green

center

Pansy

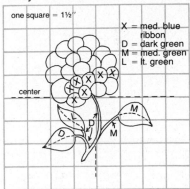

one square = 1½"

X = med. blue ribbon
D = dark green
M = med. green
L = lt. green

center

Hydrangea

Hydrangea Pillow

To work this flower, appliqué the light blue petals around the outside of the flower head first, following the general instructions. While stitching, arrange each ribbon so the gathered edge falls toward the inside of the flower. Then add center flower petals, stitching center ribbons so that their folds overlap the gathered edges of ribbons that form the outside petals. Add medium blue petals last. Anchor folds with tiny stitches tucked underneath.

When the ribbon flower is completed, embroider the stem in satin stitches and the leaves in close herringbone stitches, following color directions on the pattern. Finish the pillow by following the general instructions opposite.

Coat both of these shaped appliqué pillows with soil-retardant spray, if desired. To clean, vacuum lightly around ribbons.

Appliqué and Stitchery—Wall Hanging

Every contemporary appliqué artist understands and appreciates the contributions of this amazing little machine to the craft.

To stitch up your own tribute to the sewing machine, make our wall hanging using a variety of appliqué and embroidery techniques. Begin with regular appliqué, add trapunto quilting, then tuck and fold other appliqués to give your machine real-life dimension. Finish with simple embroidery stitches to enhance the design.

Materials

16x22 inches black fabric
⅔ yard gray fabric
1 yard white fabric
6x20 inches orange fabric
5x5 inches tan fabric
1 yard unbleached muslin
6x12 inches black, orange, and
   tan print fabric
10x16 inches black and gray
   print fabric
15x15 inches black and silver
   metallic fabric
12 inches black middy braid
Black and tan embroidery floss
Silver metallic thread
Black sewing thread
Polyester fiberfill
Dressmaker's carbon
20-inch and 25-inch pairs of
   artist's stretcher strips
Staple gun
Wire for hanging
Picture frame (optional)

Directions

Cut a 28x33-inch rectangle from the white fabric and a 24x29-inch rectangle from the muslin. Center the muslin on the wrong side of the white fabric, leaving a 2-inch border on all sides. Machine-baste the two pieces together along the sides in a ½-inch seam. Turn and baste a ½-inch hem in the white fabric. Press.

Enlarge the pattern and center it face up on the right side of the white fabric. Lightly trace the pattern onto the fabric using dressmaker's carbon and a tracing wheel or pencil.

Cut out the pattern pieces adding a ¼-inch seam allowance and following the fabric color guide. Do not cut the white fabric for the background panels, the metallic shape on the left end of the sewing machine, or the gray and black fabric shape at the center bottom.

Using two strands of tan floss, embroider the details on the black sewing machine, following the stitch guide. Using random straight stitches, appliqué the tan, oval stitch-length indicator to the right end of the sewing machine with black sewing thread. Work all the black embroidery on the tan oval except the couching stitches down the center of the oval.

Turn and press seam allowances on gray (B), orange (C), and black/orange/tan print (E) pieces. Position the pieces on the white background and appliqué in place using black sewing thread.

Appliqué the black and silver metallic piece (H) to the left side of the machine using tiny stitches and black thread.

Cut a 5x6-inch piece of black and silver fabric. Turn the edges under ¼ inch and press. Machine-stitch ⅛-inch tucks down the long side, spacing them ½ inch apart. Appliqué the piece to the background using a neat slip stitch. Match the shape's left and lower edges to the outline shown in diagram. Trim fabric ¼ inch beyond outlines at

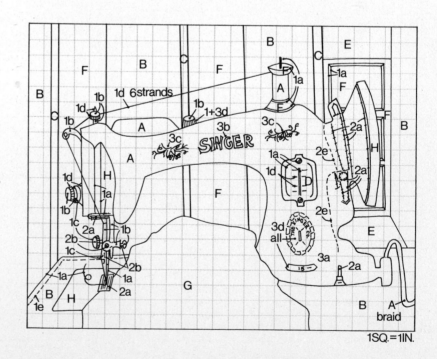

1SQ.=1IN.

upper edge and right side of shape. Slip-stitch fabric to the background along the edges.

Appliqué the sewing machine and remaining shapes to the background. To make gray and black print "fabric" under the machine's needle, slip-stitch around edges of the shape, then crumple or pleat excess fabric in center to make "folds." Slip-stitch folds in place so the fabric looks gathered.

Add dimension to the machine by trapunto-quilting some sections. Turn the hanging over to the muslin side. Cut slits through muslin beneath the sewing machine and stuff with padding until shape is gently rounded. Use an orange stick to work stuffing into small spaces, if necessary. Slip-stitch the opening.

Using two strands of floss, embroider the rest of the design, following the stitch guide, but use six strands for the thread between spool and needle. Use one strand of silver where called for.

To further contour the machine, pull the following couching stitches from the right side through the padding to the back of the hanging with tight overcast stitches: tan oval, both ends of the machine, and the silver running stitches on the right end.

Assemble stretcher strips into a frame. With right side down, center the hanging inside the frame. Beginning in the center of each side, staple the hanging to the back of the frame. Mount in a purchased frame, if desired.

Fabric Key

A   Black
B   Gray
C   Orange
D   Tan
E   Black/orange/tan print
F   White
G   Black/gray print
H   Black and silver metallic

Thread Key

1   Black floss
2   Silver metallic
3   Tan floss

Stitch Key

a   Couching stitch
b   Satin stitch
c   Stem stitch
d   Straight stitch
e   Running stitch

Reverse Appliqué—Wall Hanging

This wall hanging is a challenging project indeed—and probably not one for beginners. But if you are ready for a major undertaking, we think you will find it exciting.

Inspired by an ancient Peruvian monument built by the Incas, this "Gateway to the Sun" wall hanging is worked entirely in reverse appliqué. For this technique, pieces of fabric are stacked together and the top layers are then cut away to reveal the colors beneath. Careful planning, cutting, and stitching are essential for this work—but the unusual results are worth it.

The pattern (on page 66) is divided into five sections. Cut and stitch each one separately before assembling this 30x45-inch hanging.

Materials
Note: All fabrics are
  45-inch-wide cotton
  broadcloth
3½ yards dark blue fabric
2¼ yards purple fabric
1¾ yards gold fabric
1 yard each of dark red, light
  green, orange, and forest
  green fabric
⅝ yard cherry red fabric
½ yard pink fabric
⅓ yard brown fabric
Thread to match fabrics
Dressmaker's carbon paper
Pattern-tracing fabric
Sharp embroidery scissors (or
  other small scissors)

Directions
Enlarge the pattern on page 66, following directions on page 67. Note that there are five sections in the design. Make a separate pattern for each one by transferring each section to a rectangle of pattern-tracing fabric the same size as the fabric layers in that section (see specific directions below). Then construct each section individually before stitching it to the adjoining section. Trace the pattern lines onto the fabric layers with dressmaker's carbon. Do not cut into the pattern itself; keep it in one piece.

Work the design for each section as follows: Layer the fabrics in the order given in the specific directions that follow for each pattern. Transfer design lines to the top layer of the fabric. Adding ¼-inch seam allowances, cut along design lines to—but not through—the color indicated on the pattern. Start cuts with sharp-pointed embroidery scissors; do not start them at corners. When adding seam allowances, bear in mind that you will be cutting into the top layer or layers to reveal the fabric beneath, so add seam allowances to the top layer or layers above the color indicated on the pattern. For example, if you cut through gold and purple to blue, add seam allowances to gold and purple layers.

After cutting along outlines, pin shapes in position and set aside top layers that are completely cut away.

Appliqué shapes with thread to match the color of the fabric being sewn down. Use a regular appliqué stitch, and if necessary, trim away underlayers of fabric to reduce bulk in hems as pieces are stitched. When sewing, appliqué from the bottom layer up, stitching the topmost layer in place last.

Pattern #1 (border): Layer 1⅓ yards each of gold (top), purple, and navy blue fabric. Pin together every 6 inches along the edges.

Pin the border pattern on top of the fabric and transfer design lines with dressmaker's carbon. Add ½-inch seam allowances to outer edge and cut it through all layers. Ignoring the purple triangles in the outer border for the moment, trace and cut the inner and outer edges of gold to the color indicated on the pattern. Add ½-inch seam allowances. Trace and cut inner edge of border through purple and blue layers, this time adding ¼-inch seam allowances. Set aside inner rectangles for cutting out smaller pieces.

Trace squares on gold, add seam allowances, and cut out to purple layer only (do not cut into purple fabric). With a ruler and chalk or pencil, mark an "X" on each purple square between diagonal corners. Cut along the "X" to blue, extending cuts ½ inch under gold layers at corners (see the how-to diagram on page 64). This completes the triangle shapes that accent the squares.

Starting with the bottom left square, fold under the two horizontal purple triangles, extending the one at the outer gold edge ⅝ inch into the blue margin, as shown in the photograph (the base of the triangle will be under the gold fabric). Turn under the seam allowance and pin. Fold under triangles in remaining squares as indicated on the pattern, extending one triangle into the blue border on alternate squares. Pin. To sew, clip ¼ inch into gold corners, turn under seam allowance on triangles, and stitch, starting ¼ inch under the gold edge. Next, turn under gold hems and stitch. Turn under seam allowance on inner edge of border and baste.

continued

Reverse Appliqué—Wall Hanging *(continued)*

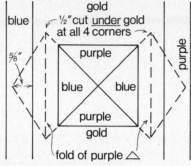

Cutting border triangles

Pattern #2: Cut the following nine colors into 18x22-inch pieces and layer in the order listed: brown (top), dark red, pink, light green, orange, navy blue, forest green, purple, and cherry red. Lay the pattern over the fabric and pin along the top edge.

Trace the lines of the *lower half* of the design, including the line in the center along the top of the brown area. Cut to dark red along this center horizontal line, adding the seam allowance to the brown fabric. Make remaining cuts in lower half of the pattern by working from left to right: make vertical cuts between sections first, then lift the strip of fabric between cuts and make horizontal cuts. For example, cut the slanted lines at the lower left of the pattern *to—but not through—*the navy fabric. Lift the wedge of fabric, revealing the navy blue beneath, and trim it along the horizontal *(top)*, leaving the seam allowance on the brown fabric.

After cutting and pinning the lower half of the design, replace the pattern over the lower half and pin across lower edge. Unpin the top. Fold the pattern down and remove the upper half of the brown fabric—above the center horizontal line that was cut first. Pin the brown fabric in position. To make remaining cuts, pin pattern over fabric, trace the line to be cut, fold the pattern down and cut to the color indicated. Remove the fabric above the line and pin the shape. Do not cut triangles yet.

In triangular area, cut horizontal lines first, starting in the middle of the design above first row of triangles. For example, with pattern over fabric, trace line at top of lowest row of triangles. Fold down pattern and cut along this line to orange (add seam allowance). Remove dark red fabric above orange; replace pattern and trace the next horizontal line. Continue as above.

After tracing and cutting horizontal lines, cut curved line at top of pattern, adding ¼ inch seam allowance. Then replace pattern, trace vertical lines separating center section of triangles, and trace triangles onto color strips. Cut through vertical lines to purple, extending cuts ½ inch under brown layer. Pin together all layers of the cut segment (in the center) and cut to purple along the bottom of the center segment ½ inch under the brown layer. Remove the pinned, cut segment (purple shows through).

Turn the cut segment upside down and pin it back into its original place. The top edge of the segment (dark red) should be even with the top edge (forest green) of the color strips at each side. To make hemming easier, remove from the cut segment the pink and light green layers that are directly under the dark red layer. Pin dark red back in its original place.

Turn under seam allowances on all pieces, baste, and appliqué, starting at the top of the design and working toward the center. Trim underlayers to remove bulk as necessary. On the bottom half of the design, appliqué shapes in place from left to right.

Pattern #3: Cut the following into 12x22-inch pieces and layer in the order indicated: cherry red (top), purple, light green, forest green, pink, navy blue, and orange. Pin layers together on short sides. Pin top edge of pattern to top layer.

Trace outlines of cherry red arches, adding seam allowances to cherry red. Pin along arches and cut away fabric to purple. Discard cherry red fabric except where pinned. To cut remaining shapes from the pattern, work from the top of the design to the bottom.

Starting with purple, cut each successive layer as follows: Trace the V-shaped outline of the triangle in the upper arch onto the fabric. Cut the *top layer of fabric only* along the outline, adding seam allowances and extending the cut ½ inch *under* the cherry red arches. Pin the triangle in place. Next, trim away the top layer, except for the pinned triangles, between the upper and middle arches.

To cut the multicolored center arch, trace the outline of the shape and pin the shape in position. Add seam allowances and cut away the remaining top layer, extending the cut ½ inch under the cherry red bands. Discard excess fabric. Repeat this procedure for the multicolored arch at the bottom of the pattern.

Work through all three arches with one color at a time, starting with purple and working to the bottom layer (orange). Then, turn under all seam allowances, clipping corners and curves. Appliqué all shapes in place with thread to match fabrics. Stitch the bottom layer (orange) first, then work toward the top layer (red). When hemming colors whose cut edges extend ½ inch under cherry red bands, continue the sewing line under the bands for ½ inch.

Appliqué pattern #2 to #3 as indicated on the pattern.

Pattern #4: Cut the following colors into 12x22-inch pieces and layer in the order indicated: forest green (top), gold, light green, dark red, brown, navy blue, and purple. Pin the top edge of pattern #4 to the layered fabrics. Work from left to right.

Mark outline of forest green mountain (including circles) and cut to layer beneath (gold). Trace around larger circle onto a separate scrap of pink fabric, adding ½ inch all around. Cut out pink and tuck into circular cutout as shown. Then trace outlines on remaining mountains on the left and cut top layers as indicated.

For mountains on the right, fold layers already cut (dark green to dark red) out of the way. Then cut brown, blue, and purple layers. Pin layers as they are cut. Appliqué all layers in place, starting on the right and working toward the left. Appliqué design #3 to design #4 along lines indicated on pattern.

Pattern #5: Cut the following colors in 12x22-inch pieces and layer in order indicated: light green (top), orange, forest green, navy blue, dark red, gold, and purple. Pin the pattern along the left edge of the fabric layers.

Trace outline of light green ray onto fabric. Pin and cut. Discard remaining top layer. Mark and cut successive right-hand rays in the same way. When they are pinned and cut, unpin pattern from left edge; repin along top edge of layers of fabric.

Trace outlines, pin, and cut rays on left of pattern starting with orange layer at bottom. After all are cut, appliqué in place beginning with left-hand rays. Appliqué pattern #4 to #5.

To assemble the hanging, appliqué the border to the center of the design. Turn the hanging over and trim excess fabric beneath each pattern area, leaving ¼-inch seam margins. Cut blue backing to size and stitch to front, right sides together, leaving an opening. Turn, press, and hand-quilt along border as shown in the diagram at right. Sew curtain rings to upper back for hanging.

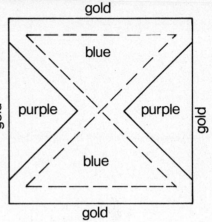

Quilting border triangles

Color Key (for pattern on page 66):

G	Gold
PL	Purple
N	Navy blue
B	Brown
O	Orange
LG	Light green
P	Pink
FG	Forest green
DR	Dark red
CR	Cherry red

continued

Reverse Appliqué—Wall Hanging *(continued)*

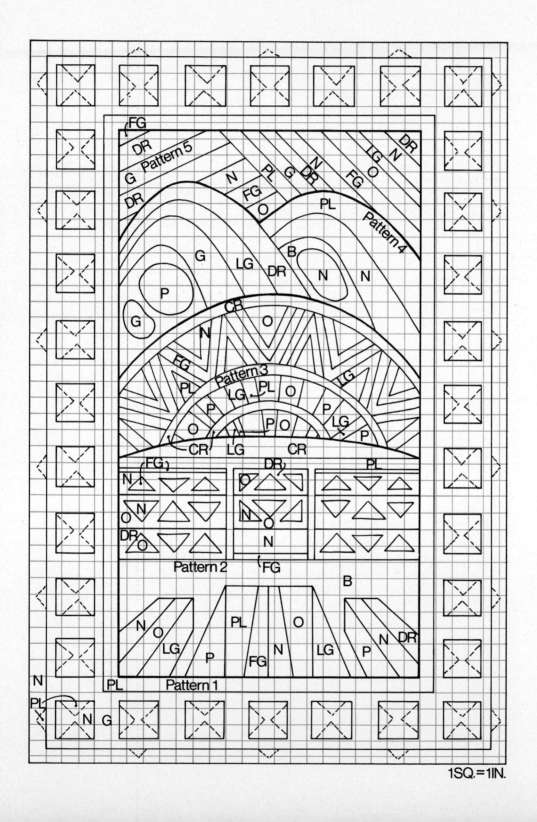

1SQ.=1IN.

Enlarging and Transferring Designs

When working with a pattern that needs to be enlarged or reduced and then transferred to fabric, choose the method that best suits your needs.

Enlarging and Reducing Designs

Patterns with grids — small squares laid over the design — are enlarged by drawing a grid of your own on tissue or brown paper, following the scale indicated on the pattern. For example, if the scale is "one square equals 1 inch," you will need to draw a series of 1-inch squares on your pattern paper to enlarge the drawing to size.

First count the number of horizontal and vertical rows of squares on the original pattern. With a ruler, mark the exact same number of rows of larger squares on the pattern paper.

Number horizontal and vertical rows of squares in the margin of the original pattern. Then transfer these numbers to corresponding rows.

Begin by finding a square on your grid that corresponds to a square on the original.

Mark your grid wherever a design line intersects a line on the original grid. (Visually divide every line into fourths to gauge whether the design line cuts the grid line halfway or somewhere in between.)

Working one square at a time, mark each grid line where it is intersected by the design. After marking several squares, connect the dots with a continuous line, following the contours of the original, as shown in the top and center diagrams at right. Work in pencil so you can erase.

Patterns without grids can be enlarged if you know any one of the dimensions of the final pattern. Draw a box around the design, making sure corners are square. Then draw a diagonal line between two corners.

On the pattern paper, draw a right angle, extending the bottom leg to the length of the new pattern. Lay the original in the corner and, using a ruler, extend the diagonal. Then draw a perpendicular line between the diagonal and the end of the bottom line, as in the lower diagram.

Divide the original and the new pattern into quarters, and draw a second diagonal between corners. Number the sections, and transfer the design.

Transferring Designs

Dressmaker's carbon paper and a tracing wheel or pencil are easy to work with. Use carbon as close to the color of the fabric as possible (yet still visible), placing it face down between fabric and pattern. Trace around design lines, using enough pressure to transfer them to fabric.

A hot transfer pencil also works well if it is kept sharp so design lines do not blur. Trace the outlines of the design on the *back* of the pattern. Iron the transfer in place.

A blue lead pencil is effective on light-colored, lightweight fabrics. Tape the pattern to a window; tape fabric over it and trace the pattern, making dotted lines instead of solid ones.

Basting is an efficient way to transfer design lines to dark, soft, highly textured, stretchy, or sheer fabrics. Use this method whenever those suggested above will not work.

Draw the pattern on tissue paper and pin it to the fabric. Hand- or machine-baste around design lines. Tear away the paper and proceed with the project. Remove basting.

When design lines are faint, regardless of the method used, trace over them with chalk.

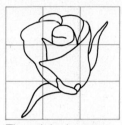

The original pattern

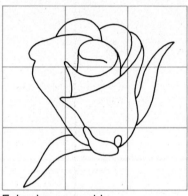

Enlarging on a grid

Enlarging without a grid

Patterns from Quilts

Because appliquéd quilts have been popular in America for generations, we have included a collection of traditional patterns for you to make. Some, like this tulip design, combine appliqué with pieced patchwork, while others are entirely appliquéd. And some patterns are easy to stitch while others are more complex. So whatever your level of skill, we think you will find a design to challenge your creativity. Directions for our tulip quilt begin on the next page.

70

Tulip Basket Quilt *(shown on pages 68 and 69)*

This traditional tulip basket pattern is a combination of pieced patchwork and appliqué. First make the baskets by piecing triangles of red and green fabric and filling them with appliquéd flowers.

Appliqué the motifs onto the blocks on the diagonal. Then set blocks together with white triangles around them and add a graceful appliquéd border. Our finished quilt measures 72x90 inches.

Materials
15 yards white cotton (front and backing)
3¼ yards green cotton
1⅜ yards red cotton
½ yard yellow cotton
Quilt batting
Thread to match fabrics

1SQ.=1IN.

Directions
Enlarge the pattern and cut out pieces, adding ¼-inch seam allowances and referring to photograph for colors. Cut stems on the bias. Turn and baste seams on stems, leaves, and flower pieces.

Cut eighteen 14½-inch white squares; appliqué 12, leaving 6 plain. For outside edges of top, cut ten 14½-inch right triangles, with longest edge on straight grain of fabric. For corners, cut four 14½-inch triangles with one short edge on the straight grain.

Piece together triangles in the tulip basket first, pressing seams to one side. Turn and baste seam allowance around basket; position it on white block so square becomes a diamond. Baste. Turn under seam allowance on basket handles and baste to block.

Pin stems in place, add leaves, and position flowers. Assemble each flower individually, starting with the bottom layer (green) and working out (yellow, red, green). Baste and appliqué.

To assemble the top, set white squares between appliquéd ones, using ¼-inch seams. Edge with white triangles, following directions above. Stitch an 8½-inch-wide white border to the top. Appliqué stem, leaves, and tulips to border, as shown. Assemble quilt with backing and batting, following directions opposite. Quilt, and then bind edges with 2½-inch-wide red bias strips.

Quilting Tips

Once you have selected a design for appliqué, check the finished dimensions of the quilt you plan to make. If you wish *to change the size of the quilt*, do so in one of three ways: alter the size of the blocks, making them smaller or larger; increase or decrease the number of blocks in the quilt; or change the width or the number of border strips around the entire quilt or along two sides. Then draw a small sketch of the quilt as you intend to make it.

After making the master pattern for the quilt block, number or letter the separate shapes to cut for appliqué and mark each shape with the number of pieces to cut. For example, for each block of the rose wreath quilt shown on pages 74 and 75, cut three shapes—the rose, flower center, and leaf. You will need 4 roses, 4 centers, and 20 leaves; note this on the master pattern. Also mark and number shapes for the border design if your quilt will have one.

Cut a sturdy template for each pattern piece from cardboard, sandpaper, or plastic lids. Do not add seam allowances to templates, but do add grain lines if they are important for your pattern.

Cut pattern pieces individually. With a pencil, lightly outline the template on the face of the fabric. The penciled line becomes the fold line for the appliqué. Leave at least ½ inch between shapes to allow for ¼-inch seams. If templates become worn around the edges from tracing, cut new ones. After cutting appliqués, sort them according to shape and keep them in order by stringing them together, as shown in the top diagram at right.

Cut stems for appliqué as long bias strips because they can be curved easily. Be sure to add seam allowances. Keep strips handy and simply cut off the length needed for a particular stem.

Turn under raw edges of appliqués and baste along the fold. Then assemble quilt blocks, following the instructions for your particular project. When appliqués overlap more than ¼ inch, trim excess fabric from the lower shape to reduce bulk and eliminate shadows.

Assemble the quilt top by stitching adjoining blocks together into rows, using ¼-inch seams. Then stitch rows together and add border strips if they are part of the design. Press seams to one side. Next, cut and piece backing fabric to size.

Assemble the complete quilt by laying out the backing fabric, face down. Smooth a layer of quilt batting on top and add the quilt top, face up, on top of that. Make sure grain lines are straight and corners are square. Pin and baste the three layers together, starting in the center and working toward the corners and sides, as shown in the lower diagram at right.

Anchor the layers together permanently by tying or by hand- or machine-quilting. For tying, mark the quilt at intervals of 3 to 8 inches; use pearl cotton, yarn, or crochet thread to take a small stitch through all layers, knotting the ends of the thread. For quilting, use commercial stitch patterns, motifs from books, or your own designs. To outline-quilt, stitch parallel to the appliquéd motifs ⅛ to ¼ inch from the edge of the appliqué. Add additional rows parallel to the first one. To quilt in a diamond pattern, stitch in parallel rows across the diagonal on the quilt; cross these rows with diagonal rows in the opposite direction.

Bind the raw edges of the quilt with narrow bias strips sewn to the edges. Or, fold the edge of the backing fabric over the edge of the quilt top, turn under the seam allowance, and hem it to the face of the quilt, being sure to cover all raw edges.

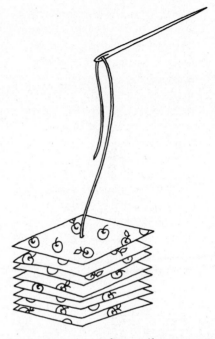

Stringing pieces for sorting

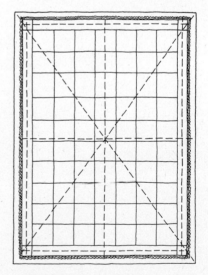

Basting layers together

Aunt Mary's Rose Quilt

Simplicity of design adds much to the charm of old quilts — especially when they are beautifully and expertly quilted in a variety of patterns that enhance the motif. Aunt Mary's Rose Quilt — a variation of the Rose of Sharon motif — is just such a design. Each of the nine blocks is appliquéd with a large rose and four graceful buds. The blocks are then set together with pink and white borders to make a quilt 79 inches square.

Materials

Note: All fabrics are 44 or 45 inches wide
9½ yards white or off-white polished cotton
⅝ yard green cotton
½ yard medium pink cotton
1¾ yards light pink cotton
Thread to match fabrics
Quilt batting

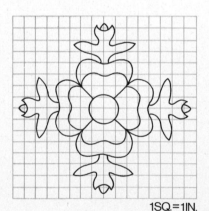

1 SQ.=1 IN.

Directions

Enlarge the pattern below at left and cut cardboard, sandpaper, or plastic templates for each of the pieces. Transfer the patterns to fabric and cut out, adding ¼-inch seam allowances.

Turn under the raw edges on the pattern pieces, clipping curves and corners. Baste.

From the white fabric, cut nine 17x17-inch blocks. Fold them in half vertically and press. Fold in half horizontally and press. Position appliqués on the blocks, centering the rosebuds and centers of the petals on the large flower on folds of the blocks. Pin and baste appliqués in position. Then, with thread to match fabrics, appliqué pieces in place.

When all blocks are appliquéd, cut six 3½x17-inch pink strips. Using ¼-inch seams, sew two strips between three blocks to make a row. Press seams to one side. Assemble three rows.

Cut four pink strips 3½x56 inches (measure rows to verify dimensions). Stitch two strips between three rows and one each at the top and bottom of the quilt. Cut two pink strips 3½x61 inches (measure to verify dimensions) and sew one to each side of the top. Press seams to one side.

For the border, cut two white strips 9x62 inches (approximately) and sew to the top and bottom. Cut two white strips 9x79 inches (approximately) and sew to the sides of the quilt. Press seams to one side.

Cut batting and backing fabric to size, and assemble the entire quilt, following directions on page 71. Baste the layers together and quilt, referring to the photograph for suggestions or using a design of your own.

After quilting, bind the raw edges with 1½-inch-wide bias strips cut and pieced from the remaining white fabric.

Rose Wreath Quilt

Made in Ohio in 1868 by Sarah Elliott, this beautiful quilt features the rose—one of the most dearly loved of appliqué motifs. Here it is worked into a wreath and accented with leaves. And the wide strips of plain fabric that separate the appliqué blocks have been heavily embellished with elaborate quilting.

The elegant handiwork in this quilt is a true inspiration to contemporary quilters.

Materials

9½ yards 44-inch-wide white
    cotton fabric
1 yard red cotton fabric
5½ yards green cotton fabric
¼ yard orange cotton fabric
White quilting thread
Quilting needle
Quilt batting
Quilting frame (optional)
Cardboard
Tissue paper
Hard lead pencil
Artist's knife

Directions

This 78-inch-square quilt is made of nine 14-inch-square appliquéd blocks separated by 7-inch-wide plain strips. A narrow green border and a wide white one, appliquéd with blossoms and buds, frame the central design. To make the quilt a different size, see the suggestions on page 71 before you proceed.

Enlarge the patterns for the block and border, opposite, to size. Transfer the pattern pieces to cardboard, sandpaper, or plastic templates. Cut pieces as indicated on the chart, turn under the seam allowances, and baste. Stitch orange centers to the red blossoms. For the vines, cut and piece 1-inch-wide bias strips. *Add ¼-inch seam allowances around all pattern pieces as you cut them out.*

For each block, cut a 14½x14½-inch white square. Fold the square in quarters and press. Mark a circle 10 inches in diameter in the center of the block for the green ring.

Position four flowers on the folds, then cut green bias strips to fit between them along the circle. Tuck the raw edges of the strips under the blossoms, and pin leaves in place as shown on the pattern. Baste all the pieces and then appliqué the entire design in place using small appliqué stitches. Complete 9 blocks.

When appliquéing bias strips in curves, sew down the inner edge of the curve first, then stretch the outer edge a bit as you appliqué it in place, so the curved piece will lie flat, without puckering.

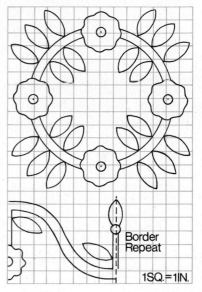

Border
Repeat

1SQ.=1IN.

To assemble the quilt top, cut six 7½x14½-inch white strips. Sew a strip to each side of an appliquéd block, then sew an appliquéd block to the second side of each strip, making a row of three blocks with two white strips between them. Assemble three rows.

Next, cut two white strips 7½x56½ inches (measure the length of the rows you've sewn together to verify dimensions). Sew a strip to each side of an appliquéd row, then sew the other appliquéd rows to the strips, for a top about 56 inches square.

Cut two green strips 2½x56½ inches (approximately) and sew them to opposite sides of the square. Then cut two strips 2½x60½ inches (approximately) and sew to top and bottom. Or, cut all strips about 60 inches long, sew to the central square, and miter corners.

Cut two white border strips 9½x60½ inches and sew them to opposite sides of the green border. Finish with two 9½x78½-inch strips sewn to the top and bottom. Or, cut four 78½-inch strips, sew them to the green strips, and miter the corners.

Appliqué the border design as shown in the photograph, above. Baste the vine in place first, then position and baste the stems, leaves, blossoms, and buds. Appliqué everything in place.

Press the finished quilt top on the wrong side over a padded board so you don't flatten the appliquéd pieces. Then assemble the entire quilt, following instructions on page 71. After quilting, bind the edges with narrow strips of the remaining green fabric.

Blue Grove Quilt

One way of making a pattern for appliqué is to cut it from folded fabric—the same way children cut snowflake designs from folded paper. This technique is characteristic of Hawaiian quilts and gives them their distinctive look.

This quilt, however, was made in Ohio in 1861 by Mary Grove. And since we do not know if Mary set out to make a typically Hawaiian quilt (although her motif looks much like a pineapple), we give you the complete pattern instead of just a segment. But you may still try folding the fabric to create your own "Hawaiian snowflake," following directions on page 92.

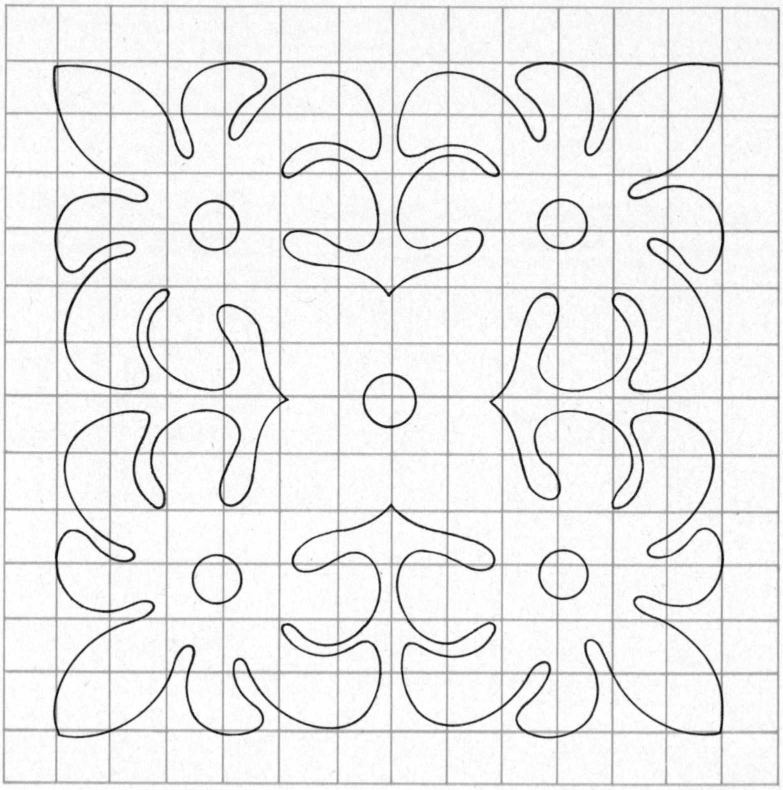

1SQ.=1IN.

Materials

9½ yards white fabric
5¾ yards blue print fabric
Quilting thread
Quilt batting
Cardboard or sandpaper

Directions

Enlarge the pattern and transfer it to a cardboard or sandpaper template. Cut 16 designs from blue fabric, adding ¼-inch seam allowances. Turn under seam allowances, clipping curves as necessary. Baste. For inner circles on pattern, snip fabric inside the circle and trim excess to within ¼ inch of design line. Clip curves, turn under the seam margin, and baste.

Cut sixteen 14½-inch squares of white fabric. Fold fabric in quarters and crease. Center a blue pineapple motif on each square, baste diagonally from corner to corner, and appliqué in place.

Assemble blocks into rows by cutting twenty 2½x14½-inch strips of blue fabric. Stitch strips between four blocks and to ends of each row (making four blocks and five strips on each row). Cut five strips the length of each row (about 66 inches) and 2½ inches wide. Set four rows together with five strips between and at the ends.

For the border, cut two white strips 3½x66½ inches (approximately) and sew to top and bottom of quilt top. Cut two white strips 3½x72½ inches (approximately) and sew to sides of top. Cut and piece ⅞-inch-wide bias strips for the border. Turn under the seam allowances and appliqué to the white strip in a cable design.

Complete the final assembly of the quilt, following directions on page 71. Quilt either in diagonal rows, as shown, or follow the outline of the motifs. Bind edges with remaining blue fabric.

Rose of Sharon Quilt

Rose motifs are a popular appliqué design. And this one—the beautiful Rose of Sharon pattern—is an especially attractive although somewhat elaborate rendition. To make a quilt like the one pictured here (about 82 inches square), you need nine 28-inch blocks. If you're not up to making an entire quilt, stitch just one square to make a dramatic pillow or wall hanging.

Because of this pattern's size and number of pieces, it is easier to stitch together the appliqués that make up the roses first, before pinning anything to the background fabric. You may use a blind stitch instead of the regular appliqué stitch to give your appliquéd roses an attractive puffed look.

Materials
13 yards 36-inch-wide white
    cotton
3¼ yards green cotton
2 yards red cotton
1¾ yards pink cotton print
½ yard yellow cotton print
Thread to match fabrics
Quilt batting

Directions
Enlarge the pattern, opposite, and transfer it to tissue paper to make the master pattern. Then, using carbon paper and a pencil, transfer the pattern to cardboard and cut out a template for each pattern piece. Do not add seam allowances to cardboard templates.

Referring to the photograph for colors, trace around the cardboard templates onto the fabrics with a hard lead pencil, outlining the number of pieces needed for a complete block: four large leaves, eight small leaves, and petals and centers for one large flower and eight small flowers. If the edges of the templates become worn, cut new ones. Cut bias strips of green fabric for stems; they curve easily without puckering when appliquéd. Add ¼-inch seam allowances to all pieces when cutting.

Turn under and baste a ¼-inch hem in the yellow print flower centers and in each of the petal pieces that make up the roses; clip curves as necessary.

Make the large flower first. Pin and baste the center of the flower to the smallest petal piece. Then pin and baste the remaining petal pieces together, taking them in order of size and color. When the entire flower is formed, appliqué the pieces together and remove the basting stitches. Repeat this stacking and basting procedure for each of the small flowers; then appliqué each layer. Use a blind stitch for the appliqué work.

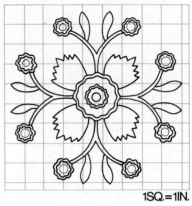

1 SQ. = 1 IN.

Cut a 28-inch square of white fabric for each block. Fold it in quarters and press, making sure creases are visible when the square is opened. Position the large rose over the center of the square; baste. Next, pin the four longer stems along the creases, curving them as indicated on the pattern. Add large leaves around the central flower, tucking the raw edges of the leaves and stems under the flower. Check the position of all the pieces against the master pattern by laying the tissue paper over the fabric block; make any necessary adjustments in their location. Pin and baste the pieces in position, using the master pattern as a guide.

Next, pin and baste the remaining short stems, leaves, and small flowers. Check their position against the master pattern. Then appliqué everything in place. Complete eight more appliquéd blocks (for a total of nine).

To assemble the quilt top, sew three large blocks together into a row, using ¼-inch seams. Press seams to one side. Then stitch three rows together into the finished top.

Assemble the quilt with a layer of batting and backing cut to size, following the directions on page 71. Quilt in the pattern of your choice. To finish, cut and piece 1½-inch-wide green bias strips to go around the quilt. With right sides together, stitch bias binding to quilt top in a ¼-inch seam. Turn under ¼ inch on remaining raw edge, and whipstitch to back of quilt.

Turkey Tracks Quilt

Turkey tracks is a pattern that combines appliqué and pieced patchwork. This old favorite is simple to stitch, and requires just a few pieces for each block.

An experienced quilter will enjoy this design, too: our 66x98-inch quilt features 60 blocks set together so the motif runs across the quilt on the diagonal. Half of the quilt blocks are simply left plain to allow you a showcase for your quilting skills.

Materials

10 yards 45-inch-wide white
    cotton (top and back)
3 yards light green cotton
1 yard green print fabric
Thread to match fabrics
Quilt batting

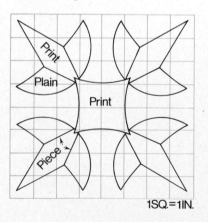

1SQ.=1IN.

Directions

Enlarge the pattern below. Using cardboard, sandpaper, or plastic lids, cut templates for the central (print) square and the two shapes that make up the track design. Do not add seam allowances to the templates. Next, trace the patterns onto the fabrics for appliqué, leaving at least ½ inch between outlines to allow for ¼-inch seams. Cut out appliqué pieces.

From the white fabric, cut sixty 8½x8½-inch blocks. Set 30 of the blocks aside; leave them plain. Appliqué the remaining 30 blocks with the turkey track motif.

To make the design for each block, piece the plain tracks to each side of the center (diamond-shaped) track in a ¼-inch seam. Press seams to one side. Piece four sets of tracks for each block. Next, turn under the seam allowance around the outer edges of the tracks, clipping the seam margin as necessary to make the edges lie flat; press and baste. Turn under the seam allowance on the central square, clipping the curves, and baste along the fold.

To assemble each block, fold a white square diagonally into quarters; press. Also fold the center appliqué piece into quarters diagonally; press. Position the center piece on the block, matching the folds, and pin. Position tracks at the corners of the center piece, as shown in the diagram, tucking the lower edge of each track slightly under the corner of the center piece. Pin and baste all the appliqués in position. Whipstitch the entire motif to the background. Assemble 30 blocks in the same way.

To assemble the quilt, arrange plain and appliquéd blocks into ten rows, with six blocks in each row. Alternate the plain and appliquéd blocks so the turkey-track blocks make diagonal rows across the top of the quilt, as shown in the photograph. Using ¼-inch seams, stitch blocks together into rows. Press seams to one side. Then stitch rows together to make the central portion of the top.

To make the border, cut two 9¼-inch-wide strips of white fabric the *length of the sides* of the quilt. Stitch one to each side of the top in a ¼-inch seam. Cut two 9¼-inch-wide strips of white fabric the *width of the quilt* and stitch one to the top of the quilt and one to the bottom. Measure carefully and then mark and cut shallow scallops around the outer edge of the quilt, as shown in the photograph. (The rim of a large round dish or tray is handy for marking scallops.)

When the quilt top is finished, press and assemble it with batting and backing fabric cut to size, following directions on page 71. Baste all the layers together.

Mount the quilt in a frame, if desired. Quilt the appliquéd blocks with rows of outline stitching on each side of the seam lines of the appliquéd design. Quilt the plain blocks with feather wreaths or a design of your own choosing. Quilt the border with rows of scallops, spacing them about 1¼ inches apart. When marking quilt patterns, use a hard lead pencil.

When quilting is finished, trim the back of the quilt to match the front along the edges, if necessary. Cut and piece 1¼-inch-wide bias strips of light green fabric to use for binding the edges of the quilt. Using a ¼-inch seam allowance, sew the binding strip to the front of the quilt. Clip curves and corners. Then turn under the ¼-inch seam allowance on the remaining edge of the binding, fold it over the raw edge of the quilt, and whipstitch it firmly to the back so the scalloped edge has a finished binding.

Dresden Plate Quilt

Quilt lovers everywhere will recognize this classic Dresden plate pattern—a favorite among quilters for years.

To make this design, first piece sections of the plate, and then appliqué the entire motif to the background fabric. Careful cutting and stitching are important to make the appliqué lie flat and smooth. We recommend that you make a sample block before cutting the pieces for the entire quilt.

Materials

12 yards 45-inch-wide white or
    off-white fabric
Assorted fabric scraps (see note
    below)
Queen-size (81x97 inches) quilt
    batting
Thread

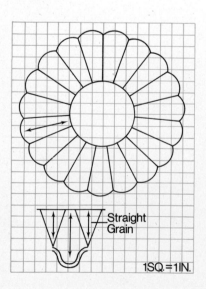

Straight
Grain

1 SQ.=1 IN.

Directions

Note: Our 79x97-inch quilt is composed of twenty 17-inch-square appliquéd blocks. The plate design has 19 wedges in it. To determine the amount of fabric needed for wedges, plan to cut 18 plate wedges from ¼ yard of fabric, or 36 wedges from ⅓ yard of fabric. Cut 14 border wedges from ¼ yard of fabric, or 28 wedges from ⅓ yard of fabric. To make a quilt the same size as ours (with 20 blocks), cut 380 plate wedges and 117 print border wedges.

Enlarge the pattern below and transfer it to tissue paper. This is the master pattern. Without adding seam allowances, trace the wedge pattern onto cardboard, sandpaper, or a plastic lid and cut it out with an artist's knife or razor blade, keeping edges straight.

Make a sample block first. Cut 19 wedges from different fabrics. Trace the pattern onto the fabric for each wedge, leaving sufficient margins to allow for ¼-inch seams. Be sure to trace and cut pieces with the straight grain of the fabric running down the center of the wedge, as indicated on the pattern. When the edges of the template become worn, make a new one.

Piece the wedges by hand or machine as shown on the pattern, using ¼-inch seams. *But leave ¼ inch unsewn* at each end of each wedge so the inner and outer edges of the plate can be turned easily when the design is appliquéd to the square. Gently press all seams to one side, being careful not to stretch the fabric.

When the plate design is assembled, pin and baste a ¼-inch hem in the inner and outer edges of the circle. This makes it easier to appliqué the plate patterns to the white blocks.

Cut a 17½-inch-square background block from white fabric and center the plate motif on it, checking its position against the master pattern. Pin and baste the design in place.

To appliqué, whipstitch the inside edge first, then the outside edge, making sure the pattern lies flat and smooth. If it does not sit correctly on the block, make adjustments in the seams between the pieces and, if necessary, in the pattern for the wedge. If the block is satisfactory, cut wedges for the remaining 19 blocks and piece and appliqué them to the background blocks, following directions for the sample block. Cut the wedges carefully so they are all the same size.

To assemble the quilt top, stitch four blocks together into a row, using ¼-inch seams. Make five rows, then stitch the rows together. Press all seams to one side.

To make the border, cut 109 white triangles and 117 print border wedges, making sure the straight grain of the fabric runs down the middle of each piece. Except for the corners of the quilt, piece the wedges and triangles alternately, as shown in the photograph at right. For the corners, piece three border wedges together. With right sides together, sew the border to the edge of the quilt in a ¼-inch seam. Press the seam to one side. Cut and piece 1-inch-wide white bias strips until they measure 13 yards. Set aside.

Cut backing fabric and batting to size and assemble the entire quilt, following directions on page 71. After basting, quilt in the patterns shown in the photograph at right, or in a design of your own. After quilting is finished, bind the edges of the quilt with the bias strips. With right sides together, baste and then stitch the binding strip to the front of the quilt in a ¼-inch seam. Clip curves and corners, then fold strip in half. Turn under ¼ inch on remaining raw edge and slip-stitch to the back of the quilt.

Creative Appliqué

As you have seen, appliqué is much more than an exciting challenge —it also is a creative craft. Even basic appliqué allows you to fabricate unique patterns and designs. And as the projects in this book demonstrate, you can combine appliqué with a variety of other needlework techniques to achieve dramatic results. Now it is time to apply all the skills you have learned and demonstrate your mastery of the stitcher's art with projects like this king-size zoo bag, which combines appliqué with regular and trapunto quilting (for how-to, please turn the page). For another fun project, create the soft sculpture cubes on page 90 with six unique and different appliquéd designs. Or turn to page 88 for all the instructions for making an appliquéd portrait of your child. The sampler quilt on the final pages of our book is an album of appliqué motifs from American quilts—a legacy from the past to inspire your handiwork today.

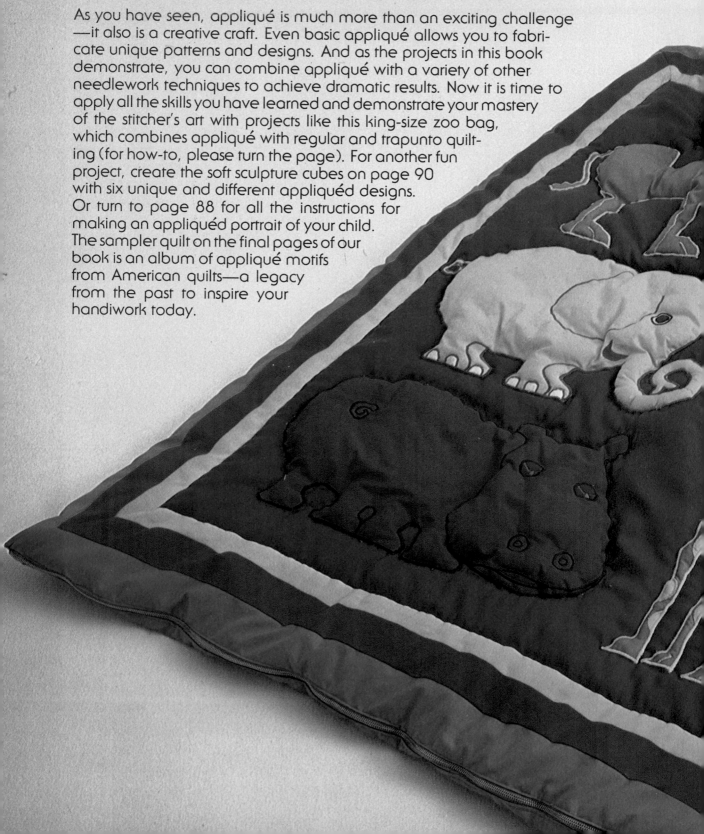

Appliquéd Zoo Sleeping Bag and Monkey Tote

(shown on pages 84 and 85)

If your children are fond of animals, they are sure to love this cozy sleeping bag, machine-appliquéd with all their favorites from the zoo. Cut the animals from the fabrics used for the border strips, assemble them and add trapunto quilting, then appliqué them to the bag.

After the bag is fully assembled with padding and lining, hand-quilt around the animals and along each border. The finished bag measures about 50x67 inches.

To make the tote bag, appliqué a monkey to fabric and stitch it onto a satchel.

Materials

3½ yards bright blue fabric
2½ yards orange fabric
2½ yards yellow fabric
3 yards green fabric
Scraps white and red fabric
6 yards 36-inch-wide fabric for lining
4 yards nonwoven interfacing
2 king-size quilt batts
108-inch zipper
½ pound polyester fiberfill
Thread to match fabrics
Blue quilting thread
Brown wrapping paper

Cut fabric as follows:
2 pieces blue, 38½x56 inches
4 pieces yellow, 2½x50 inches
4 pieces yellow, 2½x68 inches
4 pieces orange, 3x50 inches
4 pieces orange, 3x68 inches
4 pieces green, 3½x50 inches
4 pieces green, 3½x68 inches

Directions

On brown paper, enlarge designs at right. Connect ½-inch marks at edges of diagram to make a grid: 1 square equals 2¾ inches. Cut appliqués from remnants, using the photograph on page 84 as a guide. Cut basic shape from one color, then cut detail pieces to appliqué (for example, cut tiger from orange, then cut stripes from blue fabric scraps).

Pin detail pieces to animal shapes, then pin each animal to interfacing. Lightly mark non-appliquéd detail lines with pencil. (Each animal is stitched and padded before it is applied to the bag.)

Set the sewing machine on medium-width zigzag and medium-length stitch. Stitch around all appliqué details, leaving a small opening for stuffing. Next, stuff details lightly and baste openings closed. Set the machine on satin stitch (widest zigzag, closest stitch) and stitch over all basting lines.

Zigzag-baste along detail lines and again around outside edges of animal shapes, leaving an opening. Stuff lightly and baste opening closed. Then satin-stitch along all detail lines. Trim any excess interfacing from edges of animals.

Pin or baste animals in position on piece of blue fabric; machine-zigzag in place, then satin-stitch around all outside edges of each animal. Remove basting threads.

Cut out "My Zoo" and pin or glue in place. Satin-stitch.

Next, stitch yellow, orange, and green strips together, using ½-inch seams, to make bands for sleeping bag front and back. Make four 50-inch strips and four 68-inch strips. Press seams open.

With right sides together, pin strips to outer edges of blue center sections. Stitch, starting ½ inch from each corner. Next, miter all corners; stitch. Trim excess fabric from the mitered seams.

Place right sides of front and back pieces together, and stitch along one long side. Press open.

Cut lining fabric into three pieces, each measuring 34x68 inches. Stitch all three pieces together, making one piece that is 68x100 inches long. Press seams open.

With right sides facing, pin the lining and sleeping bag cover together along the top and sides. Stitch across the top and down 10 inches from the top on both sides. Turn to the right side and press.

To pad the bag: Slip two layers of batting into the bag and pin them to the wrong side of the lining. Trim the batting so it is ¼ inch narrower than the lining. Baste the batting to the lining, and then pin the bag cover to the lining and batting.

Press outer seam allowances on the cover and lining to the inside. Open the zipper. Place the bottom of the zipper at the bottom of the bag's center seam. Pin the zipper in place between the lining and the cover. Baste and then stitch the zipper in place, catching both the cover and the lining with a row of stitching. Or, apply nylon fastening tape along the same opening.

To quilt the bag: Using quilting thread and medium-length straight stitches, hand-quilt around all animals and bands. Start quilting in the center of the bag and work toward the outside edges. When quilting is finished, remove all basting.

For the tote bag: Appliqué a monkey motif onto one half of an 18x35-inch piece of orange fabric. Fold fabric in half (18x17½ inches) and stitch sides. Add a yellow lining and orange handles at the top, as shown in the photograph.

Appliquéd Portrait

Here is your chance to "paint" with fabric! Creating an appliquéd portrait of your child like the one shown here is one way to make appliqué a very personal medium. Use our pattern below, or make your own from a photographic slide following our instructions.

Materials

35x46 inches unbleached muslin, or a sufficient quantity for your portrait
½ yard small-print fabric (wallpaper) (see note below)
½ to ⅓ yard each of a variety of solid-color velvets (quilt)
½ yard brown print velvet (quilt and headboard)
½ yard unbleached muslin (pillow, arm, face)
Scrap of print fabric (nightgown)
Scraps of quilt batting
Brown sewing thread
Brown and black floss
Brown and black yarn
31- and 42-inch stretcher strips

Directions

Note: The fabrics suggested are for the portrait shown; to estimate the amount of fabric needed for your own portrait, see below.

Enlarge our pattern below or make a pattern of your own by taking a slide snapshot of your child and working from the slide. The photograph for the portrait shown was taken while the child was in bed with her favorite quilt. In your picture, you may wish to include a toy, blanket, or some other dearly loved possession of your child. Take several slides and poses of the child so you can select the composition you like best.

Insert the slide into a slide projector and project the image onto a wall covered with a sheet of white paper the same size as the finished portrait (ours is 31x42 inches). Tape the paper to the wall with masking tape so it does not shift, and work in a darkened room so you can easily see the lines in the photograph.

With a soft lead pencil or felt-tip pen, draw the lines of the composition onto the paper (be sure the pen does not bleed through onto the wall). Trace the outlines of the basic shapes, such as the head, bedstead, and blanket, and then add as many detail lines as necessary to fill out the image without making it overly complicated. This is your master pattern. Copy it onto tissue paper, mark corresponding shapes on both patterns, and cut the tissue apart into the separate shapes and pattern pieces.

To determine fabric amounts, trace pattern pieces onto an 18x44-inch piece of paper (equivalent to ½ yard of fabric) and purchase fabric accordingly.

To make the portrait, transfer the outlines of the shapes to the muslin background fabric, allowing a 2-inch margin of fabric around the design. Cut shapes to be appliquéd from the various fabrics. Do not add seam allowances. Instead, fit pieces together like a jigsaw puzzle. Pin them in place and machine zigzag-stitch to the background for a crisp, contemporary look. Then cover outlines between appliquéd shapes (on the quilt, for instance) with lengths of yarn or embroidery floss couched with machine zigzag stitches.

If you are making the portrait shown, complete all the quilt in this way, but do not stitch along the top of the quilt. Then appliqué the "wallpaper" to the upper portion of the background. Tuck the "wallpaper" down inside the loose quilt edge, then stitch. If you are working a design of your own, complete the large areas of the pattern in the same way.

Next, assemble stretcher strips into a frame and stretch the fabric over it. Add the remaining shapes—the headboard, pillow, and nightgown—by cutting out pattern pieces and hand-stitching them in place with straight stitches worked in a zigzag pattern. Vary the length of the stitches for interest. While appliquéing the pillow in place, pad it with a small amount of quilt batting.

Cut the entire head from muslin. Then cut out hair shapes from assorted pieces of lightweight cotton, and fuse them in place with fusible webbing. When the head is complete, back it with a thin layer of batting and hand-stitch it to the composition. Finish facial features and details on head with couching and satin stitches worked in embroidery floss.

Cut out arm piece, adding ¼-inch seam allowances. Turn under raw edges and stitch in place. Tuck a small amount of padding into the arm as you stitch. Add couched floss along lines of fingers.

Soft Sculpture Cubes

These soft sculpture cubes will give your children hours of enjoyment. Imagine the fun of six separate designs appliquéd onto these stackable cubes.

Add to the excitement by making some of the appliqués "movable." Then, let your youngsters arrange the facial features and add the clothes to the appliquéd boy, for example. Or decorate the house with press-on windows and shrubs. Your kids can even design their own trees with press-on palm leaves for the beach scene.

We give you basic instructions and patterns for the cubes, and leave it to you to let your imagination go.

Materials

Four 16-inch polyurethane foam cubes

Brushed corduroy (or any similar soft fabric) in the following colors: blue, purple, maroon, rust, brown, beige, green, gold, red, and white

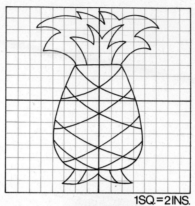

1 SQ. = 2 INS.

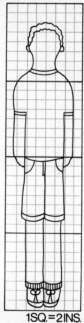

1 SQ. = 2 INS.

1 SQ. = 2 INS.

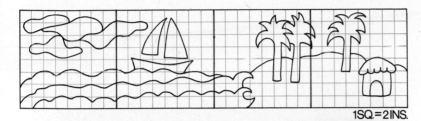

1SQ.=2INS.

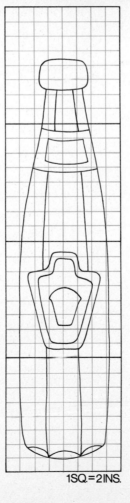

1SQ.=2INS.

Directions

For each cube, cut six 17-inch squares from corduroy. Using ½-inch seams, sew together as shown in the diagram below.

Enlarge the patterns and cut out the design pieces, referring to the photographs for colors. Add ¼-inch seam allowances to all pieces. Turn raw edges under and appliqué the pieces to the cube covers, being sure to stitch one quarter of each design to each cover.

If desired, stitch some pieces to a lining fabric, right sides together. Turn, slip-stitch openings, and sew nylon fastening tape to the back. Sew a matching strip of fastening tape to the cube cover so pieces adhere.

To assemble, fold the squares around each cube; slip-stitch together all open seams so each side is covered.

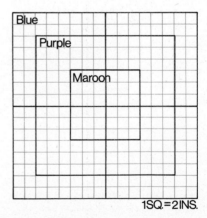

Blue
Purple
Maroon

1SQ.=2INS.

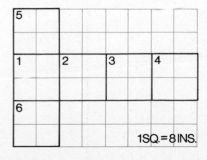

1SQ.=8INS.

Appliquéd Sampler Quilt

An appliquer's album of patterns, the quilt at right is a wonderful way to display your stitchery. Any of these 25 patterns (see pages 94 to 96) would make a beautiful quilt, pillow top, or wall hanging. All together, they present a stunning sampler of appliqué art.

This quilt is 108 inches square, but you can adjust the size to fit your own bed with our directions.

Materials

7½ yards 44-inch-wide white fabric (front)
10 yards 44-inch-wide fabric (backing)
4 yards print fabric (strips between blocks)
2½ yards green fabric (leaves and stems)
1½ to 2 yards each of 4 different fabrics for appliqués
Scraps of 2 or 3 additional fabrics in accent colors
Four 18½x18½-inch squares of print fabric for Hawaiian quilt blocks
1 yard fabric (binding)
One 120-inch-square quilt batting

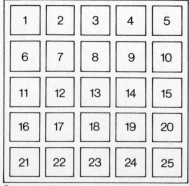

Sampler Quilt

Directions

Our sampler quilt is made of twenty-five 18-inch-square blocks separated by 3-inch-wide borders. The blocks are set into five rows of five blocks each. To make a smaller quilt, reduce the size of the blocks. For example, 12-inch blocks separated by 3-inch borders will make a quilt approximately 78 inches square, while 14-inch blocks with 3-inch borders will assemble into an 88-inch square.

Decide on the size of your quilt and enlarge the patterns for the blocks on the pages that follow, referring to the directions for enlarging designs on page 67. The scale given with the patterns is for the king-size quilt. In addition to the master pattern for each block, make a second pattern to cut apart for pattern pieces.

Preshrink all the fabric and press it smooth. Then cut twenty-five 18½x18½-inch white squares for background blocks.

For all the blocks except the four Hawaiian cutouts in the corners of the quilt, cut appliqués from fabrics, referring to the photograph for colors. Add ¼-inch seam allowances to all pieces. Cut bias strips of green fabric to use for stems. Turn under the seam allowances on all pieces, clipping curves as necessary, and baste.

Pin the appliqués for each block in place, checking their position against the master pattern. Baste and then whipstitch each appliqué to the background fabric.

Make the Hawaiian cutouts in the corners of the quilt in one of two ways. Transfer the design as it is shown in the patterns on the following pages to the fabric with dressmaker's carbon and a tracing wheel. Do not add seam allowances to the patterns. Cut the fabric along the pattern outlines, turn under raw edges ¼ inch, and baste. Or, cut out the motif the same way you would cut a paper snowflake. Fold the print fabric in half vertically and press; fold it in half horizontally and press again. Fold it diagonally (into a triangle); press all folds. Then mark the pattern, drawing a line through the vertical center of the design. Next draw a line from the center into one corner, segmenting ⅛ of the motif. Lay the segment of the motif over the folded fabric, matching the straight grain of the fabric to the vertical center of the pattern, and the bias fold of the fabric to the diagonal on the pattern. With sharp scissors, cut around the design through all layers of fabric. Open up the cutout motif, turn raw edges under ¼ inch, and baste along the fold. Center the motif on the white block, pin, baste in position, and appliqué.

When all the blocks are assembled, arrange them according to the placement diagram at left for stitching into rows. For each row, cut four 3½x18½-inch strips and sew them between five blocks using ¼-inch seams. Press seams to one side. Assemble five rows with five appliquéd blocks each.

To assemble rows into the quilt top, cut six 3½x102½-inch strips (measure the length of the rows to verify dimensions). Sew a strip between each row and one each at the top and bottom of the quilt. Finish by stitching one 3½x108½-inch strip (approximately) to each side of the quilt. Press seams to one side.

To make the back of the quilt, sew together three lengths of 44-inch-wide fabric. Press the seams open and trim off the selvages, as they are hard to quilt through. Assemble and complete the quilt, following directions on page 71. After quilting or tying, bind the raw edges of the quilt in the color of your choice.

continued

Appliquéd Sampler Quilt *(continued)*

Hawaiian Cutout   1SQ.=1IN.

Hollyhock Wreath   1SQ.=1IN.

Rose of Sharon   1SQ.=1IN.

North Carolina Rose   1SQ.=1IN.

Hawaiian Cutout   1SQ.=1IN.

Tulips   1SQ.=1IN.

Ohio Rose   1SQ.=1IN.

Wild Rose   1SQ.=1IN.

English Flower Garden   1SQ.=1IN.

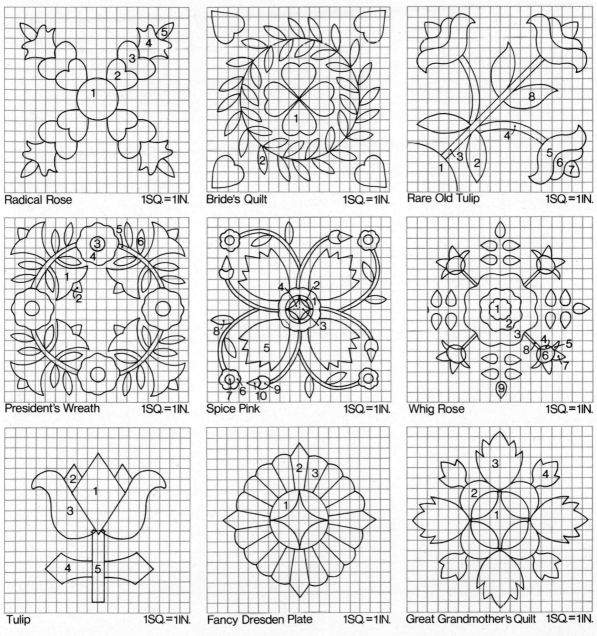

Radical Rose   1SQ.=1IN.

Bride's Quilt   1SQ.=1IN.

Rare Old Tulip   1SQ.=1IN.

President's Wreath   1SQ.=1IN.

Spice Pink   1SQ.=1IN.

Whig Rose   1SQ.=1IN.

Tulip   1SQ.=1IN.

Fancy Dresden Plate   1SQ.=1IN.

Great Grandmother's Quilt   1SQ.=1IN.

continued

Appliquéd Sampler Quilt *(continued)*

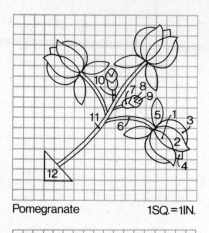

Pomegranate   1SQ.=1IN.

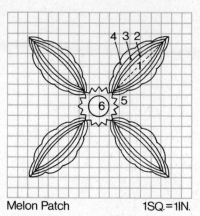

Melon Patch   1SQ.=1IN.

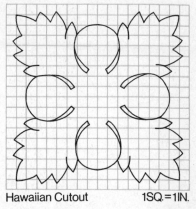

Hawaiian Cutout   1SQ.=1IN.

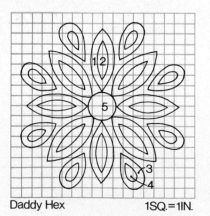

Star Flower   1SQ.=1IN.

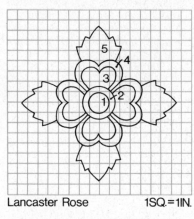

Lancaster Rose   1SQ.=1IN.

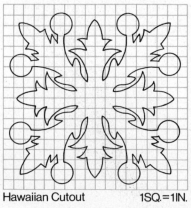

Daddy Hex   1SQ.=1IN.

Hawaiian Cutout   1SQ.=1IN.

Designers

Margot Blair	50-51
Linda Brock	24-27
Joan Cravens	52-53, 58-59
Patricia Gardner	18-19
Susan Hesse	28-29, 30-31
Becky Jerdee	34-35, 36-37, 60-61, 88-89
Marge Kerr, for QUILTS IN THE ATTIC, Denver, Colorado	92-96
Carol Lee Knutson	10
Jean LemMon	14
Sherry LeVine	12-13
Carol Martin	54, 55
Jill Mead	84-87
OCEAN BEACH QUILTERS, San Francisco, California	32-33, 38-41, 48-49
Martha Opdahl	62-66
Alice Proctor	11
Cinda Shambaugh	20-21
Mimi Shimmin	4-5, 22-23
Suzy Taylor	46-47
Ciba Vaughan	56-57
Judith Wagstrom	15
Mike Wigg	16-17
Joy Wulke	90-91

Acknowledgments

Living History Farms
  Des Moines, Iowa
Mary Barton
Heidi Horten
Mary Jane Linderman
Judy Murphy
Mike Wigg